5 MINUTES
with the PSALMS *and the*
WISDOM BOOKS

"In the chaos of the classroom, it is easy to lose sight of what matters most. *5 Minutes with the Psalms and the Wisdom Books* is a great addition to the desk of the busy teacher, who even when busy, needs to be still and rest in the presence of the Lord. I love the brevity, clarity, wit, and wisdom of these reflections written by teachers in the trenches. Each one is a reminder of the most important job we have as educators: to bring our students close to the heart of Jesus and simply be with him. It is not only a valuable resource but a great gift to any and all who find themselves with a classroom of students yearning for the Truth."

Katie Prejean McGrady
Freshman theology teacher and author of *Room 24*

"The smart teacher provides mere facts while the wise teacher adeptly applies such information to invite students to consider the awesome truth of God and the enduring realities of eternity. This book will draw any teacher to a finer appreciation and respect for the Lord's timelessly divine wisdom, thus allowing educators to better profess and proclaim the Good News of Jesus Christ for their students' ultimate well-being."

Justin McClain
Theology teacher and author of *Called to Teach*

"In their service to the Gospel as educators, Catholic teachers are on the front lines of the New Evangelization. These reflections by Catholic teachers offer daily help to those who share in this important mission to keep their focus on Jesus Christ, Word and Wisdom made Flesh, and so embody his truth and love to those they serve."

Most Rev. Kevin C. Rhoades
Bishop of Fort Wayne-South Bend

5 MINUTES
with the PSALMS *and the*
WISDOM BOOKS

Spiritual Nourishment for
Busy Teachers

edited by

Lou DelFra, C.S.C., *and* Ann Primus Berends
of the Alliance for Catholic Education
University of Notre Dame

AVE MARIA PRESS AVE Notre Dame, Indiana

© 2017 by the Alliance for Catholic Education

Founded in 1865, Ave Maria Press is a ministry of the United States Province of Holy Cross.

www.avemariapress.com

Paperback: ISBN-13 978-1-59471-709-3

E-book: ISBN-13 978-1-59471-710-9

Cover image © RMN–Grand Palais / Art Resource, NY.

Cover design by David Scholtes.

Text design by Katherine Robinson.

Printed and bound in the United States of America.

Library of Congress Cataloging-in-Publication Data is available.

Contents

INTRODUCTION

[Thus says the Wisdom of God:]
*When [the L*ORD*] set for the sea its limit,*
*   so that the waters should not transgress [the*
*   L*ORD*'s] command;*
*When [the L*ORD*] fixed the foundations of earth,*
*   then was I beside [God] as artisan;*
*I was [the L*ORD*'s] delight day by day,*
*   playing before [God] all the while,*
Playing over the whole of [God's] earth,
*   having my delight with human beings.*

PROVERBS 8:29–31

On that day, as evening drew on, Jesus said
to the disciples, "Let us cross to the other side."
Leaving the crowd, they took him with them in
the boat just as he was. And other boats were
with him. A violent squall came up and waves
were breaking over the boat, so that it was
already filling up. Jesus was in the stern, asleep
on a cushion. They woke him and said to him,
"Teacher, do you not care that we are perishing?"
He woke up, rebuked the wind, and said to the
sea, "Quiet! Be still!" The wind ceased and there
was great calm.

MARK 4:35–41

When I was a middle school and high school teacher in Philadelphia, I spent my after-school hours in one of my favorite pastimes—coaching! I loved it, so I never missed a season. I coached soccer or football in the fall, basketball in the winter, and baseball in the spring. It was a whirlwind of activity every afternoon. Amid this whirlwind, however, I discovered one constant, invariable rule across all seasons and sports: "Keep your eye on the ball."

The physics are obvious enough. The ball is moving, and so are we—often wildly. A batting coach once told me that 172 muscle motions—from the cocking of the elbow to the shift of weight from back foot to front to the forward motion of the front elbow to the snap of the wrist at contact—must be executed properly to consistently hit a baseball. In tennis, because the whole body is moving, the number jumps to 243. If you're a golfer, don't let anyone tell you that you are not an athlete because one golfer has claimed that 352 muscle motions are needed to consistently drive a golf ball straight. (Though golfers do seem more prone than other athletes, short of fishermen, to exaggerate a bit . . .)

But here's the point: in the midst of—and, in fact, precisely because of—all these motions swirling around, there is an absolute imperative that something remain still in the center if anything productive is to result. *Our eyes must not move*; they must not leave the ball. To put it more starkly: we can execute every motion of a swing correctly, but if we take our eyes off the ball, if there is not a still point in the center of our motion, we will only ever hit the ball by sheer luck.

And this brings me to wisdom, the focus of this collection of spiritual reflections for teachers, who spend their days perpetually in motion and in the midst of countless whirlwinds!

The book of Proverbs tells us that wisdom was present with God at the creation of the world, and so wisdom understands the workings of the movements of the universe and playfully delights in all its wonders. "When [the LORD] set for the sea its limit, so that the waters should not transgress [the LORD's] command . . . then I was beside [God] as artisan . . . playing before [God] all the while." What an image, especially for the ancient Jewish community, for whom the seas were the very embodiment of chaotic movement and mystery. In the midst of it all, wisdom delightedly plays over the waters as the Creator gives their chaotic surges and roaring waves firm boundaries. In the midst of the movements of the universe is the still point untroubled by all the commotion—wisdom.

I imagine St. Mark the Evangelist had this image in mind as he composed his narrative of Jesus and the disciples crossing the Sea of Galilee in their boat one evening. As they sailed, an event well-known to a teacher of any experience level suddenly transpired—seemingly out of nowhere, an utterly unprepared-for, utterly disruptive whirlwind engulfs their boat. Mark vividly renders it a "violent squall." Suddenly, what began as a communal journey toward a desired goal (imagine here your more-or-less ordered homeroom just before the first bell) is jolted by forces well beyond their control.

For the disciples, this force was the storm, encountered terrifyingly without a Weather.com forecast, GPS, or life preserver "stowed beneath your seat in the unlikely event of a water landing." For us educators, these forces can range from something as simple as a fire drill to something as complex as a student's turbulent home life manifesting in a classroom outburst. From something internal to ourselves (fatigue, lack of preparation, a lesson plan gone awry) to external tempests (an uncooperative colleague, an unsupportive administrator, an unappreciative parent waiting in the hallway), these storms, large and small, can threaten our classroom community's journey on any given day—just like that squall did for those disciples in their boat on the Sea of Galilee.

How vital, then, to our ministry as educators is Mark's poignant memory of what saved that day: in the middle of the whirlwind, something remained still, unmoved, setting limits on the sea—Jesus, "in the stern, asleep on a cushion." Jesus is here, the living, human incarnation of wisdom. It is he to whom Proverbs refers. It is he who was present when the universe was created—"all was created through him, all was created for him" (Col 1:16). It is Jesus Christ who was present when the seas and their boundaries were set and so who understands the origin and limit of every storm. It is he, then, who can sleep, delighting in the swells and waves, experiencing what terrifies the disciples as instead the comfort an infant feels in a rocking cradle. Jesus is the still point within all of life's storms. Jesus is our wisdom.

In the midst of the sometimes exhilarating, sometimes debilitating whirlwinds of our lives as educators, what is our still point, the part of us that never moves? What centers us and weathers all, even finding delight and peace underlying the ripples and riptides?

I can't help but think here of one of my favorite images from Dante's *Divine Comedy*. As Dante begins his trip into Paradise, he encounters a soul in one of the outer heavenly rings. The souls in Paradise are arranged in concentric circles, leading up to God, who exists in the center. Dante questions the soul on the outer ring as to whether she doesn't wish to be in one of the higher rings of heaven, even closer to God. I imagine this soul's eye fixed immovably on God, the still point, the Beatific Vision. And she is able to reply with perfect contentedness, unshakable tranquility, and pure joy, simply, "His will is our peace."[1]

So the will of God—expressed at once so perfectly and so humanly in Jesus—is something that centers, and makes sense of, all our activities. It is to be convinced that we are not educators by random chance or even by our own initiative (even if it appears that way at times) but rather that we enter the daily whirlwind of education because God calls us there. To know that God's will is at the center of all our daily activities—a center that can bring meaning to our motions, calm to our storms, and even allow us to delight in the swells and tides—frees us to say with the soul in Dante's Paradise, "I don't wish to be anywhere else, because God wills me here."

If we keep our eyes on Christ as the still point, the many activities of our lives can have meaning and, instead of fraying or exhausting us, bring us joy and peace. This is one thing it means to live with Christ's wisdom at the center of our lives.

Or here is another image that can help us. It's a sentence, an insight that comes from Dag Hammarskjöld, the former secretary-general of the United Nations: "We all have within us a center of stillness surrounded by silence."[2] Here is a person who lived in the middle of the whirlwind! The secretary-general of the United Nations sits within the storms of the world—the wars, the famines, the refugee migrations. In Hammarskjöld's diary, discovered only after he died, he reveals his spiritual journey and struggles as well as how deeply he was influenced by the wisdom of the medieval mystics.

Can you imagine discovering stillness surrounded by silence in the center of your soul while being secretary-general of the United Nations? It is hard enough coming to this realization as an educator! But this should encourage us: if Dag Hammarskjöld could find Jesus sleeping on a cushion in the stern of the boat, then so, perhaps, can we.

To live our calling as educators with wisdom is to give ourselves this daily reminder: "All the activities and even whirlwinds of my life can exhaust me, and my ministry can lose its meaning and coherence, if I lose sight of my still point—Jesus, the beginning and end of all the movements of my life, of all the movements of my students' lives, of all the movements of the universe."

This book is a collection of reflections from the Wisdom literature of our scriptures—the books of Job, Psalms, Proverbs, Ecclesiastes, Song of Songs, Wisdom, and Sirach. These reflections are written by a faith-filled community of educators in the University of Notre Dame's Alliance for Catholic Education (ACE)—teachers, principals, administrators, and members of the ACE faculty and pastoral team who help form ACE's teachers and principals. We are a community that strives to keep Christ the Teacher as the center of our focus, the center of our ministry as educators, and the still point amid the inevitable whirlwinds of this exhilarating call to teach.

We hope these reflections can serve as a daily encouragement to fellow educators. Together, we seek to cross the seas of life with the students whom God has entrusted to us. Together, we will endure many whirlwinds along the way. But let us do so remembering that the wisdom of Jesus Christ is at the center of us all, guiding all things back to him. Let us never take our eyes off of him!

Fr. Lou DelFra, C.S.C.
Director of Pastoral Life
Alliance for Catholic Education (ACE)
University of Notre Dame
Notre Dame, Indiana

REFLECTIONS

COMMUNITY OF "JOBS"

JOB 4:3–4

Look, you have instructed many,
and made firm their feeble hands.
Your words have upheld the stumbler;
you have strengthened faltering knees.

These are the words of Job's friend Eliphaz, as spoken to Job following a disastrous series of events in which Job loses his livestock, servants, and children within one day. While any one of these calamities would be enough to shake a person's confidence in God, Job ultimately chooses to bless the name of the Lord.

Any life dedicated to serving God will be filled with struggles and tribulations, teaching of course not excluded. Teaching is extremely demanding of one's emotional, mental, and physical capacities. I have discovered, however, that being surrounded by a community of "Jobs" has helped me find the ability to persevere each day. The strength formed in a group of friends committed to a common goal—especially a spiritual one—is one of the most inspiring and powerful blessings I have received. Friends bring us to completeness by helping us recognize and rise above our shortcomings.

Throughout our lives we experience moments when we need the perspective and support of a "Job" and moments when we are called to be a "Job" for others. As a teacher, I have found this to be particularly true. God calls us to see Christ in our students and to support them in their times of despair, which can range from failing a test to being denied admission to a college to the loss of a parent or loved one. A ministry of presence is an easily missed aspect of our vocation, drowned out by the chaos of lesson planning, grading papers, and disciplining students. But this ministry is central to our mission.

Today, let us be thankful for those in our lives who are a source of strength for us and for those for whom we are called to be sources of strength. Let us be thankful for Job and bless the name of the Lord.

David Lee
Latin and Science Teacher
Our Lady of Mercy Catholic High School
Fayetteville, Georgia

KNOWLEDGE AND
WONDER AND AWE

JOB 26:7–10

[The LORD] stretches out Zaphon over the void,
and suspends the earth over nothing at all;
[The LORD] binds up the waters in the clouds,
yet the cloud is not split by their weight.
[The LORD] holds back the appearance of the full
moon
by spreading clouds before it.
[The LORD] has marked out a circle on the sur-
face of the deep
as the boundary of light and darkness.

A few years back, I was amazed by the trick of a street magician in which the card I had picked somehow ended up in my pocket. Baffled and curious, I searched the Internet that night to unveil the trick's secret. I found a detailed description of the illusion and, like the card in the magician's hand, my initial sense of wonder slipped through my fingers, replaced by a deflated feeling of disenchantment.

People in the time of Job had myriad explanations, mostly based on myth and tradition, for how the earth stayed in place, why the moon waxed and waned, and what formed the clouds. It was not until many centuries later that many of these stories were replaced conclusively by evidence-based, scientific explanations. For some people, unfortunately, these explanations eclipsed their amazement at God's creation.

But for me, knowing nature's secrets differs dramatically from uncovering the magician's sleight of hand. Gravity, this constant and measurable attraction that holds planets and moons together in a system, or the earth's water cycle, which forms billowing clouds that are nothing more than vapor—these become even more marvelous when understood.

Using science and math to predict the exact phases of the moon or to learn what lies at the horizon need not lead us to disenchantment with God. No, science and math even more deeply reveal to us, and instill within us, the wonder of creation and its Creator.

As a teacher of science and of science teachers, I often look to the gifts of the Holy Spirit in which knowledge and wonder and awe stand together (Is 11:2–3). The gift of knowledge—about the Big Bang, evolution, how the earth orbits the sun—belongs with the gifts of wonder and awe. Our ability both to make sense of the world and to find inspiration in this knowledge is but one more reflection of the grandeur of God.

Matt Kloser
Faculty
Alliance for Catholic Education
University of Notre Dame
Notre Dame, Indiana

GOD ON TRIAL

JOB 38:1–5

*Then the L*ORD *answered Job out of the storm*
and said:
Who is this who darkens counsel
with words of ignorance?
Gird up your loins now like a man;
I will question you, and you tell me the
answers!
Where were you when I founded the earth?
Tell me, if you have understanding.
Who determined its size? Surely you know?
Who stretched out the measuring line for it?

At the end of their entrance interviews, many new teachers ask whether there is a greatest challenge that beginning teachers typically experience. "I think there is," I have come to reply, "and it results from falling in love."

I go on to explain to surprised faces that this challenge has nothing to do with navigating romantic love and everything to do with the healthy love that teachers develop for their students. Of course, vexing parents, defiant students, and piles of grading can require the patience of Job. But what most unsettles and even enrages teachers is to learn from the depth of their love for their students that so many suffer profoundly—even at a tender age—from grief, abuse, neglect, poverty, or sickness.

The problem of suffering lies at the heart of the book of Job. We all know the story—Job, faithful servant of God and richly blessed in life, loses everything as the object of a divine wager. And it turns out that Job is really not so patient after all, especially as his so-called friends blame him for his own misery. So Job demands a hearing; he puts God on trial, as it were, to explain why the innocent suffer. Does he not speak for all of us?

The book of Job, to me, offers no satisfying answer or consolation so much as raw honesty. This encounter between God and Job doesn't sugarcoat the most urgent question we face as believers: Why must the good suffer? God's answer "out of the storm" reminds Job and all of us of our puny human limitations before the all-powerful Creator.

But Job comes before Jesus, and Jesus changes everything. Scripture's final wisdom must wait until the life, death, and resurrection of Jesus. Only in the extraordinary lessons of the Cross, where God takes on the fullness of human pain, and in the garden outside the empty tomb, where—in contrast to the deafening

voice from the storm—Jesus tenderly calls Mary Mag-
dalene by name, do we find the infinitely satisfying
if still mysterious answer that there is mercy and joy
beyond our imagining, beyond the foundations of the
earth, for ourselves and those we love.

John Staud
Faculty
Alliance for Catholic Education
University of Notre Dame
Notre Dame, Indiana

GOD IN LITTLE WAYS

JOB 38:25–27

Who has laid out a channel for the downpour
and a path for the thunderstorm
To bring rain to uninhabited land,
the unpeopled wilderness;
To drench the desolate wasteland
till the desert blooms with verdure?

My mother's friend lost her young daughter to a sudden illness. Vibrant and full of life in the evening, the young girl was found dead the next morning. To support her friend, my mom wrote her a note: "Many people are probably consoling you by telling you this loss is according to God's plan or that God is using this as a trial to make you stronger. Don't listen to them. While we don't know why young innocents suffer, still we understand that God may use all the little ways God knows to give your daughter back to you."

Job laments his plight, including the loss of his own children, atop an ash heap and endures lengthy "consolations" from his friends. He demands an answer specific to his problem, but God, speaking from the storm, gives him a universal and cosmic response.

11

God lists many of the wonders in creation—hawks, horses, and lions combined with constellations, tidal waves, and hailstorms—to form an awe-inspiring picture of our world. In revealing such immense majesty, God helps Job realize that the components of this storm—each one a divine creation that communicates God's presence—are in fact all around him. Job comes to understand that God is present in the world in many little ways and that Job needs only to look up from the ash heap to see the God he so desperately needs.

Perhaps there's a lesson to be learned here for our daily trials in the classroom. We sometimes feel as though God ignores our cries for relief. But the book of Job reminds us that God is not hiding beyond the chaos of the everyday. God, instead, is in the midst of the mess, charging it with love, hoping that any piece of that maelstrom will help us recognize God's constant presence. Often these little ways are enough to cause the desert within us to bloom with verdure. When we find God in the mayhem of our days, we, too, can proclaim with Job, "I know that my Redeemer lives" (19:25).

Thomas Spring
Middle School Religion and Social Studies Teacher
Saint Vincent Ferrer School
Vallejo, California

TIGHTLY LACED CONTROL

JOB 42:1–3

Then Job answered the LORD and said:
I know that you can do all things,
and that no purpose of yours can be hindered. . . .
I have spoken but did not understand;
things too marvelous for me, which I did not know.

When I sit down to get ready for school in the morning, an indicator of how I feel about the day ahead is how tightly I tie my shoes. If I am anticipating a long day, or if I am particularly anxious about something on the schedule, I tie my shoes very tightly, as if—to use biblical terms—I am girding up my loins for the battle ahead. On these mornings I usually catch myself planning how I might accomplish everything that I need to do and worrying that something won't go exactly as I had planned. The tightness of my laces is a small way for me to exert control.

Inevitably, as the hours pass, the laces loosen. This happens gradually, and it accompanies a subtle release of the control that I try to maintain over the day. A coworker's unexpected knock on the door or a student's surprisingly insightful question remind me that no matter what I had anticipated, I am ultimately not the one in charge. God has a plan for each day and works through us to accomplish it. No matter how tightly we hold on and try to accomplish the things *we* want to accomplish, we experience the spiritual reality that Job proclaimed: "No purpose of [God's] can be hindered." Then our grasp loosens—an act Job rightly describes as marvelous.

When I take off my shoes at the end of these tightly tied days, I feel freed from the burdens and anxieties that knotted me up in the morning, and I am filled with thanksgiving and awe. I think of the good things that happened, both big and small, anticipated and unanticipated, and wonder at all that took place.

We cannot know all the ways that God works through and around us. We cannot understand all the plans God has for us and those we are called to teach. What we call "uncertainty" is sometimes just a begrudging confession that God is ultimately in charge of this space of things we do not understand. May the Spirit grant us the grace to tie our shoes loosely and allow God's wonderful acts to unfold!

Brogan Ryan, C.S.C.
Former Middle School Math and Religion Teacher
Seminarian
Moreau Seminary
University of Notre Dame
Notre Dame, Indiana

Choosing Our Path

Psalm 1:1–3, 6

Blessed [are those] who do not walk
    in the counsel of the wicked,
Nor stand in the way of sinners,
    nor sit in company with scoffers.
Rather, the law of the Lord is [their] joy;
    and on [God's] law [they] meditate day and
        night.
[They are] like a tree
    planted near streams of water,
    that yields its fruit in season;
Its leaves never wither;
    whatever [they do] prospers. . . .
Because the Lord knows the way of the just.

Psalm 1 debunks the worldly notion that walking in step with God leads to a life of boredom, drudgery, and encumbrance. God's laws were not meant to weigh us down with guilt and bondage but rather to show us the path to freedom and delight.

The psalmist kicks off by abruptly calling us to make a decision: To what will we say no and to what will we say yes in terms of how we think, act, and live? The original meaning of the word *blessed* here literally means "Oh the happiness!" or "Oh the joyfulness!" What we decide to do—or not to do—will lead us to joy.

So, happy is the one who says no:

"No, I'm not going to listen to the advice of those who don't put God first."

"No, I'm not going to hang with those who take me down the wrong path."

"No, I'm not going to let someone else give me the script for what I value."

And, happy is the one who says yes:

"Yes, I will seek God's counsel."

"Yes, I will hang with those who keep me on the right path."

"Yes, I will make God's Word the script for what I value."

"Oh the joyfulness!" for those who make God their focal point, who take their cues and influences from God's Word, who saturate their lives with God's wisdom. They—we!—will be like trees planted in lush surroundings next to a beautiful flowing stream, rooted, stable, and fruitful. And note that the fruit we produce is not for us to eat but for others to enjoy. Oh the joy for us when we stand strong for God in selfless sacrifice for our students and colleagues, family, and friends. All the while, God watches over us. God is with us wherever we sit, stand, sleep, run, walk, and go.

As the Lord said, "Stand by the earliest roads, ask the pathways of old, 'Which is the way to good?' and walk it; thus you will find rest for yourselves" (Jer 6:16). We will find the path of freedom and delight.

Kole Knueppel
Faculty
Alliance for Catholic Education
University of Notre Dame
Notre Dame, Indiana

Perfectly Loved

Psalm 8:4–6

When I see your heavens, the work of your fingers,
the moon and stars that you set in place—
What [are human beings] that you are mindful
of [them],
[sons and daughters] that you care for [them]?
Yet, you have made [them] little less than a god,
crowned them with glory and honor.

It is 2:30 in the morning. My daughter, Nora, is four days old. She is decidedly not tired. Desperate to lull the newborn nestled in my arms to sleep, I instinctively begin whispering sweet nothings into her tiny, peach fuzz–lined ears: "Mommy loves Nora so much! Do you know why Mommy loves Nora? Mommy loves Nora because . . ."

My sing-songy voice trails off. "I love you because . . . I love you because . . . I love you. I love you because you exist. I love you because you are." Tears well in my eyes as I kiss the top of her sweet-smelling head. At ninety-six hours old, she has given me no reason to love her beyond the basic fact of her existence—yet it is this very existence that makes my heart overflow. She is pure gift. I love her because she is.

As a teacher—formerly of middle schoolers and now of college undergraduates—I occasionally encounter students whom, because of bad attitudes or questionable behavior, I struggle to see as gifts made in the image of God. There have even been times when I have thought, "Goodness, this class would be so much easier to teach if Larry were not in it." But my experience as Nora's mom has begun to transform the way I see my students, especially the most difficult ones. Nora is a constant reminder to me—even while crying in the middle of the night—of the inherent worth and dignity, and thus lovability, of all human beings.

As she grows older, my daughter will undoubtedly do many things that frustrate, anger, and perplex me, things that will call me to new levels of forgiveness. But none of that will alter the fundamental truth of her existence, the realization that took my breath away that sleepless night: that Nora is a person "crowned with glory and honor," perfectly loved by God and infinitely worthy of my best attempts at loving. And if she is, then so is every child, even the one crying out in the back of my classroom.

Susan Bigelow Reynolds
Former Middle School Language Arts and Social Studies Teacher
Doctoral Student
Department of Theology and Education
Boston College
Boston, Massachusetts

FROM GRUMBLING
TO GRATITUDE

PSALM 13:3–6

How long must I carry sorrow in my soul,
grief in my heart day after day? . . .
Look upon me, answer me, LORD, my God!
Give light to my eyes lest I sleep in death,
lest my enemy say, "I have prevailed,"
lest my foes rejoice at my downfall.
But I trust in your mercy.
Grant my heart joy in your salvation.

When we're feeling bogged down by work and other stressors in life, rattling off a list of complaints is no problem. I may not always be as eloquent (or dramatic) as the psalmist who offers the ultimatum "Give light to my eyes lest I sleep in death," but I can sure lay down some lamentations of my own.

There are days when I walk into my classroom feeling as though I just don't have it. I bear the weight of unfinished and imperfect planning and grading. I dwell on the setbacks in lesson content and student behavior that I should have resolved by now. And, perhaps worst of all, I see a glaring discrepancy

20

between my current performance and the habits and pedagogical effectiveness of the teacher I aspire to be. It all leaves me questioning, "Am I good enough?" Which, on really bad days, can deteriorate into some of the psalmist's more intense groans: "What am I doing here? Is this worth it? How long must I carry sorrow in my soul?"

Then it happens. A discussion in a class picks up, and the teacher-student relationship gels. A hallway conversation with a colleague reveals an underlying camaraderie with a joke, a word of encouragement, or a smile. A student's work exhibits not only learning and understanding but also effort and interest. Suddenly my question has been answered for me: "Yes, this is worth it! This is a blessing."

For all the time I have spent analyzing my inadequacies, I have never totally overcome any of them, and I certainly have not become perfectly passionate, confident, or holy. But as God whispers to me in little ways to turn my gaze outward and to pour myself into those around me, my dissatisfactions melt away. Opportunities for small acts of service and love replace the opportunities for doubt and criticism. Joy again overtakes me as I hear my grumblings transform into gratitude.

The psalmist rendered his lamentation powerfully, in words that give voice to my own heart's sadness at times. It is good to remember that the same psalmist also beautifully announced the remedy to such sadness: when we trust in God's mercy, our hearts will rejoice.

Brian Schwartze
Middle School Math and Science Teacher
St. Pius X Catholic School
Aurora, Colorado

GOD'S INVITATIONS

PSALM 16:11

You will show me the path of life,
abounding joy in your presence,
the delights at your right hand forever.

Think back to that moment when you first felt called to teach. Was it during childhood in the classroom of a beloved teacher? Was it later in life when learning about educational issues or through a fulfilling experience such as tutoring? Did the call evolve over time, or did it seem to come out of nowhere?

How God invited you into the teaching ministry may be mystery, but what is certain is God's presence every step of the way. Indeed, every one of us can echo the psalmist's words with confidence, "You will show me the path of life," knowing that we have the graces needed to respond to God's invitation. Joy abounds in walking the path God chooses for us.

Every day, God's invitations continue. We hear them whispered through the voices of our students and colleagues; we perceive them in classroom happenings and needs that demand attention. Our trust that God will show us the way can allow us to see each invitation as a graced opportunity for growth, joyful response, or even movement in an unexpected direction. As we enter our schools each day, we can pray with confidence, "You will show us the path of life that will bring fullness of joy!"

Whatever comes our way today, may we trust that God will guide us. May we rest in comfort knowing God accompanies us with every step taken along life's path, showing us the way to wholeness and leading us to complete joy in God's presence!

Sr. Gail Mayotte, S.A.S.V.
Faculty
Alliance for Catholic Education
University of Notre Dame
Notre Dame, Indiana

Following Our Leader

The Lord is my shepherd;
there is nothing I lack.
In green pastures he makes me lie down;
to still waters he leads me;
he restores my soul.
He guides me along right paths
for the sake of his name.
Even though I walk through the valley of the
shadow of death,
I will fear no evil, for you are with me;
your rod and your staff comfort me.
You set a table before me
in front of my enemies;
you anoint my head with oil;
my cup overflows.
Indeed, goodness and mercy will pursue me
all the days of my life;
I will dwell in the house of the Lord
for endless days.

Psalm 23 is so intricately designed. It is filled with meaning about the goodness of the Lord, our Good Shepherd, the grace that he shows us, and the compassion with which he cares for us. When I was younger, I used to think of Psalm 23 as an ode to the mercy of God. And it is. But intertwined with this is another reading whose effect is so visceral that it shakes me to my core and moves me to worship when I simply sit with each line:

In green pastures he *makes me* lie down . . .

To still waters he *leads me* . . .

He *sets a table* before me in front of my enemies . . .

God is in control in every aspect, in every way.

When leading us through quiet places—a productive school week or peaceful time spent with loved ones—the Lord is our generous provider, giving us nourishment and rest. When leading us through certain danger—challenging relationships with students or colleagues or tenuous seasons of self-doubt—God is our protector, giving us courage and comfort. And so great is our Shepherd's goodness that he gives us the choice to follow him—or not. Whether we walk along still waters or through a dark valley, our Lord longs for us to follow his lead.

That places of rest, rejuvenation, peace, and gentleness are included in the same psalm as places of danger, darkness, peril, and grief is no accident. God is present and in control when our waters are quiet and all is well in family, in community, and in job or vocation. But just as certain, God is present and in control during impoverished times, when all is not well and we stand most in need of him.

Today, may we decrease so that our Lord may increase. May we follow where our Shepherd leads, whether beside still waters or tumultuous ones. May God be our light, as the sun when it is shining highest in the sky or the moon casting a glow in the darkness. May the Lord be our shelter, where we will dwell our whole lives long.

Allison Jeter
Former Second and Third Grade Teacher
Associate Program Director
Alliance for Catholic Education
University of Notre Dame
Notre Dame, Indiana

Flawed Heroes

Psalm 27:1–2[3]

The Lord is my light and my salvation;
whom shall I fear?
The Lord is the stronghold of my life;
of whom shall I be afraid?

For the past few years, I have conducted a yearlong tournament in each of my history classes. Every week, students research designated historical figures and we discuss their merits. Finally, we vote on which contestant was most courageous.

Perhaps the whole concept of voting on one person's courage over other equally heroic actions seems a little artificial. The process, however, is much more important than the result. The tournament exposes my students to inspiring individuals who possessed different kinds of courage: spiritual, mental, or physical—often all three. But all of these heroes had weaknesses of one kind or another, too. However inspiring the stories, my students inevitably discover that every hero was a flawed human being with whom they actually have much in common. The stories of these individuals challenge my students and me to rise above excuses and strive to achieve greatness despite our weaknesses.

But is this really possible? Sometimes, in the most hectic moments of the day, I wonder how in my brokenness I can possibly be expected to constantly encourage the student who gets under my skin or firmly and cheerfully enforce rules that students hate even though they will be better for it in the long run. Then I remember the promise of this psalm: "The LORD is the stronghold of my life." With God as my strength, I don't have to do it on my own. What a relief!

God calls teachers to be daily examples of courage, a virtue C. S. Lewis called "the form of every virtue at the testing point."[4] God calls teachers to show courageous patience. Courageous empathy. Courageous charity. Courageous selflessness. Yes, we are flawed . . . but God is not. And God calls on us in the normal course of our days to live out the virtues to their testing point. God calls us not to be nice but heroically charitable. God calls us not to be giving but heroically selfless. And we can do these things even when we feel most broken and weary. For the Lord is our light, our salvation. The Lord is our life's stronghold.

Meghan Hadley
Seventh and Tenth Grade History Teacher
The Willows Academy
Chicago, Illinois

A Shift in Perspective

PSALM 34:2–4

I will bless the LORD at all times;
praise will always be in my mouth.
My soul will glory in the LORD;
let the poor hear and be glad.
Magnify the LORD with me,
and let us exalt his name together.

Bless the Lord *at all times?* Praise *always* in my mouth? We naturally bless the Lord at the end of a great school week or when students score well on a tough assessment. Praise of the Lord rolls off our tongues when we see students make breakthroughs and reach their full potential. We can't help but bless the Lord when we see students perform in the school play or watch them compete in an athletic event. Sometimes, though, the psalmist's call to unceasing praise proves to be much more challenging. How can we bless the Lord when struggling students don't progress no matter how many interventions we have tried? How can we praise the Lord after a difficult parent conference?

A student once taught me an important lesson about changing my perspective in challenging circumstances.

Our classroom in Birmingham, Alabama, overlooked a busy intersection frequented by frustrated drivers. Much to my chagrin, these drivers would often honk their horns as they waited at the light outside our window. Knowing how much this frustrated me, the student finally said, "Mr. Ryan, when they honk, they are telling other drivers that God loves them." True or not (and in this case, surely not!), this shift in perspective changed each outburst of road rage into an opportunity for me to think about God's love. A gentler viewpoint transformed moments of aggravation into moments when the praise of God could be in my mouth.

I think this is what the psalmist had in mind. He was not promising good times free of difficulty. Rather, he was reminding us that blessing the Lord at all times and keeping praise forever in our mouths—even when we have to significantly alter our viewpoint of the present circumstances—can allow us to see the crosses in our lives as gifts from God.

God has only gifts to offer. Let us look for the blessings in every circumstance, and then, together, let us magnify the Lord and exalt God's name—yes, *at all times*!

Brendan Ryan, C.S.C.
Former High School Math Teacher
Seminarian
Moreau Seminary
University of Notre Dame
Notre Dame, Indiana

In Days Full of Trouble

Psalm 34:19–20

The Lord is close to the brokenhearted,
saves those whose spirit is crushed.
Many are the troubles of the righteous,
but the Lord delivers them from them all.

The life of a teacher is hard. Planning engaging lessons; maintaining firm, fair, and consistent classroom management; grading stacks of papers every weekend; working with difficult parents; doing many things for our schools in addition to teaching—it's all hard. But there is good news! God comes to us precisely in and through the many struggles that define the life of a teacher.

These verses from Psalm 34 use words that describe educators on many days: brokenhearted, crushed in spirit, saddled with many troubles. But, as if a microcosm of salvation history, these verses also remind us that relief and respite are never far off. In fact, through our hardships God is active and alive in our days. Our small, daily sufferings are perfect opportunities for us to open our hearts and minds to the God who saves and delivers.

Consider the design of the liturgical calendar. The Church plots the course for the year, orienting the entire timetable around Easter, the day of perfect joy. Yet Easter comes after days of intense sadness and suffering. This reminds us that only after grappling with the reality of death can we experience the reward of salvation; only after persevering through anguish can we attain that ultimate joy.

St. John Paul II wrote that we are "called to share in that suffering through which the Redemption was accomplished."[5] In this light, our vocation as educators is not so different from Christ's own mission. Like him, we give of ourselves—freely, completely, sometimes painfully—so that those we serve will flourish. As Pope Benedict XVI said, "Jesus did not redeem the world with beautiful words but with his suffering and his death."[6] How beautiful it is that God can work so many miracles through all that is hard about teaching!

So we never lose hope. The Lord is always close, the psalmist says, especially during days full of trouble. And the Lord will deliver us from them all.

Patrick Boyden
Middle School Religion and Social Studies Teacher
Our Lady of Grace School
Sacramento, California

Moments of Stillness

Psalm 46:11

Be still and know that I am God!

I had never been less still in my entire life.

The first year of teaching is a time of dawn-to-dark activity: waking up early, preparing for the school day in the faculty room, adjusting plans mid-lesson, mentoring via clubs and sports, grading and planning in the evenings. My life before teaching included abundant time for quiet and contemplation. I made sure that my schedule allowed for daily Mass, frequent praying of the Rosary, weekly adoration, Bible-study meetings, and reading St. Thomas Aquinas. My life while teaching that first year stood in stark contrast, to say the least!

At the end of the fall semester, I remember talking with a priest about this radical change in my prayer life. Worry consumed me because I believed that I was no longer giving all that God deserved. The endless activity prevented me from hearing God's voice, the voice of a parent and friend whom I truly missed. The priest let me vent my concerns, and then he explained something to me. He told me that God does not ask for a life of quiet and contemplation from everyone. From most, God expects only moments of stillness. God can work wonders of grace, he said, in a single moment of stillness.

Encouraged, I began building moments of stillness into my days of activity: driving in silence to work, taking a minute or two of quiet during a planning period, reading a short scripture passage before falling asleep. My new prayer life as a teacher is often vastly different from the one that my college schedule allowed, but that need not make it any less rich.

With infinite mercy, God is willing to speak to me and comfort me even if I can offer only a few minutes at a time. I have learned to trust that God will continue to show me that he is God, bringing peace even when my life of teaching is anything but still.

Ealish Cassidy
English Teacher
St. Petersburg Catholic High School
St. Petersburg, Florida

Good, True, and Beautiful

Psalm 51:8

Behold, you desire true sincerity;
and secretly you teach me wisdom.

How does the Lord teach us wisdom? In *The Idea of a University*, Bl. John Henry Newman writes, "All that is good, all that is true, all that is beautiful, all that is beneficent, be it great or small, perfect or fragmentary, natural as well as supernatural, moral as well as material, comes from him."[7] This, I think, is how we come to know wisdom: we soak in the truth of God's being as it exists in everything around us.

I'm a middle school language arts teacher at heart, presently living the life of a graduate student. I had one of those "That's what I've been *trying* to say!" moments when I read Newman after my first year in the program. That idea—that God's goodness, truth, beauty, and beneficence can be found everywhere— bridges my experience as a teacher with my current reality as a student.

As a teacher, I wanted my students to see how everything we learned connected to other academic content and to their faith. What is it about the imagery in that poem that's got you so excited? Why is the community in *The Giver* so troublesome to you? What I hope my students learned is that they got worked up about what they were learning because they were seeing something true, good, and beautiful—something of God, in a new way. That's why the psalmist juxtaposes truth and wisdom. To see truth (or beauty or goodness or beneficence) is the beginning of wisdom.

Now a student again myself, I ask similar questions about what I'm learning and how it moves me. The response is the same: "I get worked up about what I'm learning because I am seeing something of God in a new way." The responsibility for student-me now is the same as it was for teacher-me before, the same that it is for all of us: to see God in all things and then to usher others into that reality.

The most wondrous part is that, to do this, we don't need to be great philosophers like Newman. We simply point each other toward the good, the true, and the beautiful, and together celebrate the inevitable outcome: God will teach us wisdom.

Andrea Cisneros
Former Middle School Language Arts Teacher
Doctoral Student
School of Education
University of Michigan
Ann Arbor, Michigan

Everyday
Sanctuaries

Psalm 63:2–3

O God, you are my God—
it is you I seek!
For you my body yearns;
for you my soul thirsts,
In a land parched, lifeless,
and without water.
I look to you in the sanctuary
to see your power and glory.

This psalm strikes me as particularly relevant to us as educators. Aren't many of our students like a "land parched, lifeless," or as described in another translation, "dry and weary"? Some students are parched from unhealthy home situations, low self-esteem, poor body image, feeling left out, or being bullied. Others are weary from frenetic schedules originally designed for their betterment: AP classes, sport and music competitions, volunteer work, and part-time jobs. In search of water, many turn to Facebook, Snapchat, and text messages, only to find that these oases easily evaporate into mirages.

This problem isn't limited to students. We educators become parched and weary from the stress of our multitude of responsibilities, both in school and outside it. In our desire to finish one more task on a seemingly infinite to-do list, we postpone activities that would nourish us, such as prayer, conversations with friends, nature walks, and quiet alone time. We grow dry and weary, and often don't realize it until we yell at a student in class, gossip about a boss or coworker, or ignore a significant relationship.

The psalmist realizes the only relief for his thirst is to look to God in the sanctuary. How are we to look to God, and where is our sanctuary? Of course, I would be remiss not to recommend quiet prayer time in a chapel. Do this! But our sanctuary can also be found in the everyday places and moments of our lives. We gaze on God in the sanctuary when we recognize the drops of grace sprinkled throughout our days: the "ah-ha" epiphany of a struggling student, the thank-you note from a coworker, the smile of a loved one. In these sacred moments, God waters our parched spirits with love and transforms our hearts into fertile ground.

As Christian educators, may we constantly look to God in the sanctuary and encourage our students to do the same, allowing God to prepare us for an abundant harvest of grace.

Tom Bodart, C.S.C.
Former High School Math, Religion, and Science Teacher
Seminarian
Moreau Seminary
University of Notre Dame
Notre Dame, Indiana

STORY-LOVING CREATURES

PSALM 78:1–4

Attend, my people, to my teaching;
listen to the words of my mouth.
I will open my mouth in a parable,
unfold the puzzling events of the past. What
we have heard and know;
things our ancestors have recounted to us. We
do not keep them from our children;
we recount them to the next generation,
the praiseworthy deeds of the LORD and [the
LORD's] strength,
the wonders that [the LORD] performed.

As a beginning teacher, I learned quickly that demanding my eighth-grade students' attention was a terrible way to try to start a lesson. Even now, as I teach motivated professional graduate students, beginning a class with "Listen up!" or even the more polite "May I have your attention?" rarely does the trick. Instead, whenever I plan a lesson or prepare any speaking engagement, I draw inspiration from Psalm 78. I pray about how I might make my point through story.

We human beings are story-loving creatures, and when a lesson is embedded in a compelling narrative, we are far more likely to listen and remember. Stories make our lessons stick. The psalmist knew this, and so did Jesus—the gospels can be read as a series of lessons delivered by a master storyteller.

I believe that stories are the most powerful teaching tools we have at our disposal. They are the vehicles by which values, beliefs, faith, traditions, and rituals have been passed down from one generation to the next for thousands of years. Today the most prominent touchstones of popular culture—*Star Wars*, for example—are stories. We spend billions of dollars each year consuming them via movies, novels, comics, video games, television, and other media. Indeed, the ubiquity of story in popular media may blind us to the simple power of a well-told tale. But our best stories—those of our scripture and tradition—are essential tools that have helped us keep the faith for more than two thousand years.

Whenever we are called on to teach, motivate, or persuade, we need only ask the Holy Spirit to inspire us with great tales that will illustrate our point. Whether we draw on the Wisdom literature of scripture, the parables of Christ, narratives from our own lives, contemporary literature, or a galaxy far, far away, we are better teachers when we engage our students with stories.

Christian Dallavis
Faculty
Alliance for Catholic Education
University of Notre Dame
Notre Dame, Indiana

Do the Right Thing

PSALM 86:11

Teach me, LORD, your way
that I may walk in your truth,
single-hearted and revering your name.

My oldest daughter, Lilia, is very conscientious, a characteristic that she likely shares with many firstborn children. She wants to do the "right" thing nearly all the time, and she often seeks guidance on what is right from my wife, me, or another adult. This extends from assignments in school to table manners to Lenten observances. If she runs into trouble, it is usually for overgenerously encouraging her younger brothers to do the right thing, too.

Though I was dramatically different when I was her age (unfortunately for my mother), I now am certainly drawn in a powerful way to seek God's guidance in my own life of discipleship. *Lord, just tell me what to do! I am weak. I am limited. I fall short. How can I hear your voice and know your way?*

In these moments, I take a deep breath and close my eyes to reflect on God's guiding presence in my life. Not surprisingly, I find God is teaching me all the time. I become aware, for example, of the gospel reading from the day before or maybe a snippet of the homily. I reflect on my interactions with my students, my colleagues, my friends, and my family members. I realize that God's voice is all around me, and I don't have to wait until the quiet of nightfall to hear it.

At the end of the day, perhaps my greatest challenge is not my difficulty in recognizing God's teaching, but in accepting it and living it out—and then, in my own small way, sharing it with others. Certainly, the vocation of an educator provides a daily opportunity to share God's truth with others. May we embrace this opportunity and experience deep joy in doing the right thing!

Packy Lyden
Faculty
Alliance for Catholic Education
University of Notre Dame
Notre Dame, Indiana

First, Mercy

Psalm 86:15

But you, Lord, are a compassionate and gracious God,
slow to anger, abounding in mercy and truth.

When Pope Francis opened the Holy Door of Mercy of the Basilica of St. Peter in Rome at the beginning of the Year of Mercy, he said, "How much wrong we do to God and his grace when we speak of sins being punished by his judgment before we speak of their being forgiven by his mercy. We have to put mercy before judgment, and in any event, God's judgment will always be in the light of his mercy."[8]

We are so blessed to be living at this time in the Church when the Holy Father has repeatedly invited us to open our lives to the relentless mercy of God. God wants the Church—and, by extension, us educators—to be a sign of God's maternal care for all people. In us, our students will see that God's mercy overpowers everything else. From us, our students will learn that God is not interested in retributive justice but in restorative justice—a justice that helps us sinners return to God, to return to our true selves. When God "punishes" us, God does so by loving us even more. Only that unconditional and reckless and relentless love—poured out upon us freely—will move our hearts to turn to the Lord.

How's this for unconditional love? After Jesus was unjustly condemned, hung on the Cross, and abandoned to death, he came back three days later and said, "Peace be with you. I love you." No revenge, no malice, no evil, no punishment, no retribution. Rather, "Peace be with you. I love you."

To understand how God loves us, we have to soak in this message from our risen Lord and invite our students to do the same. Then we can operate out of a worldview of trust and abundance rather than one of scarcity and fear. Fear and scarcity make both grace and mercy unimaginable and difficult to experience.

With each passing day, we can become more aware of God's love as the psalmist's words take root in our hearts: "But you, Lord, are a compassionate and gracious God, slow to anger, abounding in mercy and truth." So reckless, so relentless is God's love that ultimately we will be unable to resist, and we will finally give in to God's mercy. God always wins! May we be daily instruments of God's ultimate victory in each of our students' lives.

Fr. Joe Corpora, C.S.C.
Founder of St. John Vianney Catholic School, Phoenix, Arizona
Director of University-School Partnerships
Alliance for Catholic Education
University of Notre Dame
Notre Dame, Indiana

NIGHT PRAYER

PSALM 91:1–2, 15

You who dwell in the shelter of the Most High,
who abide in the shade of the Almighty,
Say to the LORD, "My refuge and fortress;
my God, in whom I trust." . . .
[The LORD proclaims, You] will call upon me
and I will answer;
I will be with [you] in distress.
I will deliver [you] and give [you] honor.

As a seminarian, I served as a hospital chaplain in an intensive care unit. My encounters with patients and family members alike often left me praying that God would give me the right words to bring comfort to people in great anguish and pain. I remember one patient in particular who had sustained critical injuries in a car accident and was in a coma, kept alive by IVs and a ventilator. His face was terribly bruised, and the nurse told me he probably wouldn't make it. They were keeping him alive until his family could arrive from another state and say their good-byes. "But, he might be able to hear you," she said. "You should . . . you know . . . pray with him or something."

49

As I sat by his bed, I was at a loss for words. I put my hand on his and prayed silently over him for consolation and a deep sense of God's care. Then I told him about Psalm 91.

I told him that every Sunday throughout the world, priests, religious, and some laypeople pray Psalm 91 as a part of Night Prayer, or Compline. It's a psalm of great trust in God's protection that actually imagines us as a bird in distress or a soldier approaching a hopeless battle. The Almighty, the psalmist says, will free our wings from being tangled in a net and will protect us under God's strong wings. God will be our shield in battle and our protection from harm. The Lord, promises this prayer, "commands his angels with regard to you, to guard you wherever you go" (Ps 91:11). God—our shelter, our shade, our refuge—will hold us close. We pray these words before we sleep, entrusting our lives to God's care.

I spoke the words of Psalm 91 slowly and deliberately over the hissing and clicking of hospital equipment. I stayed for a little while longer, and then I left.

The man died later that week, and while I will never know if he actually heard the words that tell of the tender love and care of God, I have often come back to this psalm in moments when the problems of my students, colleagues, family members, or my own life seem insurmountable. In those moments, I trust in God's simple yet comforting promise: "I will be with you."

Fr. Nate Wills, C.S.C.
Faculty
Alliance for Catholic Education
University of Notre Dame
Notre Dame, Indiana

DISTRACTIONS

PSALM 100:1-2

Shout joyfully to the LORD, all you lands;
serve the LORD with gladness;
come before the LORD with joyful song!

How often do we forget to be grateful for our students, colleagues, spouse, or siblings and instead wish they were different in some way? Life is filled with distractions—work, family, friendships, *living*! How often do we find ourselves distracted by the waiting e-mails in our inbox, the unreturned calls from family or friends, the lesson plans that have not written themselves, the classroom yet to be observed, or the Facebook post not yet liked?

A couple of years ago I didn't shout so joyfully to the Lord and serve the Lord with gladness. I was distracted. I got caught up in the way I thought things should be rather than the way they were. I prayed for what-ifs rather than thanking God for what was.

No one warned me about how tough my vocation as a wife would be. I promised my husband the day I said yes that I would help him get to heaven. I was mistaken if I thought that would be easy—for either of us! Yet the vocation of marriage is also the most beautiful and life-giving blessing in my life. My time of distraction in the difficulties of marriage proved to be a great and challenging call to a more Christian understanding of vocation. Beauty emerged—in the form of love, forgiveness, healing, reconciliation, grace, and happiness—the moment I embraced an attitude of gratitude as opposed to longing for things to be different.

Perhaps the lesson I learned from my vocation of marriage can be extended to our vocations as educators. Instead of getting distracted by how we wish our students or colleagues would behave, learn, or perform, let's celebrate and be grateful for who they are—children of God—and who they are called to be: God's light to the world. "Shout joyfully to the Lord, all you lands; serve the Lord with gladness; come before the Lord with joyful song!"

Amy Wyskochil
Former Fourth Grade Teacher
Director of Operations
Institute for Educational Initiatives
University of Notre Dame
Notre Dame, Indiana

Hints of God's
Boundless Wonder

Psalm 104:24, 30–31

How varied are your works, Lord!
In wisdom you have made them all;
the earth is full of your creatures. . . .
Send forth your spirit, they are created
and you renew the face of the earth.
May the glory of the Lord endure forever;
may the Lord be glad in his works!

Years ago I was on retreat in Glacier National Park with my two best friends. We went on an all-day hike up to one of the many mountain peaks. As we made our way through valleys and up the mountain, we saw every type of animal imaginable as well as wildflowers with more colors than a rainbow! The landscape, the waterfalls, and the ever-changing clouds that soared over us were spectacular.

When we got to the summit, we stopped to pray and celebrate Mass. As we read Psalm 104, we soaked up the grandeur of God's creation. We could not help but think of Gerard Manley Hopkins's famous lines:

"These things, these things were here and but the be-holder / Wanting; which two when they once meet, / The heart rears wings bold and bolder, / And hurls for him, O half hurls earth for him off under his feet."[9] Our hearts were filled with overflowing gratitude for this view of God's majesty.

Yet it struck me that among all the beauty of God's vast creation, most precious of it all is us! God so loved the world that the pinnacle of creation was humankind, and God gave us Jesus to help us dis-cover this splendor. I reflected on God's varied works and realized that my love for family and friends was also God's creation, given to me to appreciate God's magnificence in others. I learned that—beyond the animals, mountains, and clouds—there is much more God wants me to see.

I prayed for the grace to see each student and per-son I serve, work alongside, and live with in commu-nity as part of God's masterpiece. Rather than view them based on how they are different from me in ap-pearance, beliefs, or disposition, I asked for the grace to see each person as God does—as part of God's stun-ning creation.

May all of us experience this grace. As we reflect on the breadth and depth of God's creation, may we see in the people God has placed in our lives hints of God's boundless wonder.

Fr. Sean McGraw, C.S.C.
Faculty and Cofounder
Alliance for Catholic Education
University of Notre Dame
Notre Dame, Indiana

COMMUNITY CHORUS

PSALM 105:2

Sing praise to [the LORD], play music;
proclaim all [the LORD's] wondrous deeds!

The American folk group Peter, Paul and Mary, in the song "Music Speaks Louder Than Words," offers an important commentary on the significance of community: "Music speaks louder than words. When you sing, people understand."[10]

Something about music calls us beyond ourselves to enter a shared experience with others. While postmodern definitions of identity often seem synonymous with characteristics of individualism, music reminds us that we can only understand ourselves and our God within the context of community. As Christians, we know that only in community as the Body of Christ can each individual truly flourish and become the person God calls her or him to be.

Our Christian community reflects the idea that we do not live as isolated individuals. Rather, we unite to continue the incredible work of the Resurrection—God's kingdom come, on earth as it is in heaven. In liturgy, for example, we embody God's love by joining together in each element of worship. When we begin prayer with the Sign of the Cross, we enter more deeply into the relational love of God through a shared gesture. When we sing the psalm of the day, we proclaim the historical love of God through our harmony together. Through the Eucharist, we participate as a community in the life, death, and resurrection of Christ. Together we live, we sing, and we eat and drink the Lord's wondrous deeds.

In our schools and classrooms, we offer our students opportunities to engage this idea that each voice reaches its fullest potential only in chorus. We encourage academic competence, of course, but we also emphasize the importance of conscience and compassion. We try to teach our students that discipleship requires responding to the needs of others and working for the common good. Relationship marks our life as followers of Jesus Christ.

As Christian educators, we know the words of Peter, Paul and Mary reflect the deep wisdom of the psalmist's encouragement to "play music." May we always sing the song of God's love with our voices and our actions, helping our students to recognize the life that comes from community.

John Kyler
English and Theology Teacher
Mother McAuley Liberal Arts High School
Chicago, Illinois

Look Up

Psalm 121:1–2

I raise my eyes toward the mountains.
From whence shall come my help?
My help comes from the Lord,
the maker of heaven and earth.

The opening verse of Psalm 121 never fails to bring me back to experiences in my life when I have felt totally and utterly broken. In an instant, I find myself caught in the memory of a specific time and place, being physically, mentally, emotionally, and spiritually poured out and wanting nothing more than to lie on the ground, pull a blanket over myself, and stay there for a long, long time.

Whether dealing with the tragic news of a friend's unexpected death, tending to a cranky newborn on less than thirty minutes of sleep, or walking arm-in-arm with a loved one on the long and difficult journey back from depression, we all have hit the wall at some point in our lives. We have found ourselves exhausted on every level, pushed beyond every limit, and left simply raw and breathless. Indeed, during these periods of life when we might be filled with more doubt and uncertainty than faith and trust, we cry with the psalmist, "From whence shall come our help?"

Thankfully, in these hit-the-wall moments, we don't need to know what's ahead and we don't need to know how to move forward. All that we do need to know is how to look *up*: up toward the mountains, toward the heavens, toward our Creator God.

The second verse of Psalm 121 is an invitation to faith, to hope, and to trust: "My help comes from the Lord, the maker of heaven and earth." Surely, the Lord who effortlessly created every corner of the universe can mend the fabric of my torn-up self. God can pour love back into my broken heart. God can reinforce my broken spirit, help me heal, and ultimately make me stronger.

When I cannot breathe, the Lord will breathe for me. When I cannot see the future, the Lord will gently call, reminding me that the path is already set right before my feet. All I have to do is take it one breath, one step, and one prayer at a time. In our darkest moments, the Lord is our light shining on the mountaintop. God was, is, and will be waiting, patiently and lovingly, for us to simply look up.

Gina Navoa Svarovsky
Faculty
Alliance for Catholic Education
University of Notre Dame
Notre Dame, Indiana

Hushed and Calm

PSALM 131:1–2

LORD, my heart is not proud;
nor are my eyes haughty.
I do not busy myself with great matters,
with things too sublime for me.
Rather, I have stilled my soul.
Like a weaned child to its mother,
weaned is my soul.

EAT. SLEEP. REPEAT.
I had to chuckle as I walked through a coffee shop and passed by a newborn baby sleeping soundly in the arms of his mother. He was wearing a cute little onesie with these three words printed in bold capital letters: EAT. SLEEP. REPEAT. What a precious image! As a father of a newborn myself, all I can say in my own bleary-eyed way is if only it were as simple as those three words!

I love this image from Psalm 131 of a sleeping, contented baby representing a soul in stillness. Over the last few months, I have come to know the sheer excitement and precious achievement of a slumbering child, hushed and calm. In the moment of quiet that follows after having endured a good bit of fussing and fidgeting, I give eternal thanks to God for the chance to catch my breath and gaze at this embodiment of peace.

For teachers and administrators, moments of peace can often be few and far between. How do we seek them out? Where can we find the quiet that gives our souls the respite required to open ourselves to the wisdom of the Holy Spirit?

As we all barrel through the daily intensity of our vocations, let us ask for God's help to seek out the mental, physical, and spiritual space we need to enter into silence, if only for a moment, and allow the wisdom of the Holy Spirit to speak through the stillness that surrounds us. Then, our three-step school year routine—EDUCATE. SLEEP. REPEAT.—will not be tiresome but will fill us and our students with life and contentment.

Antonio DeSapio
President
Bishop Blanchet High School
Seattle, Washington

A GLOBAL CLASSROOM

PSALM 133

How good and how pleasant it is,
  when people dwell together as one!
Like fine oil on the head,
  running down upon the beard,
Upon the beard of Aaron,
  upon the collar of his robe.
Like dew of Hermon coming down
  upon the mountains of Zion.
There the LORD has decreed a blessing,
  life for evermore!

It was Christmas Eve 2015. One of my colleagues and I were coming back from a revitalizing Midnight Mass at the cathedral in downtown Dakar. We had been impressed with the turnout, especially given that Senegal is 95 percent Muslim. Craving a snack, we headed to the only place that was open, our neighborhood corner store.

As we entered, Ibrahim—the young store owner and a devout Muslim—immediately asked why we were both dressed up, and we explained willingly. Genuinely curious, he kept asking us questions about our Catholic background and suddenly wanted to know if he could attend Mass with us sometime soon. We gladly invited him to join us the following weekend. Little did I know that this humble invitation to Mass would provide the pretext for uniting us in a kind of global classroom.

Come Sunday, we all walked together to the closest church. Ibrahim seemed apprehensive until he entered the sanctuary, where he displayed a true sense of respect. Throughout the Mass, I found myself explaining to Ibrahim what exactly was happening and why. I was eager to teach him all I could. Walking back from Mass, we asked Ibrahim to tell us about his beliefs. He talked about his life and practices as a Muslim and the unique challenges he faces in a world that has seen a rise in anti-Islam attacks.

Just as we turned into our neighborhood, we heard the routine call for evening prayer. Ibrahim bid us adieu and headed to the mosque. In that moment, I felt a spiritual calm that I had not experienced for some time. Through our simple and seemingly fleeting exchange, our differences seemed to vanish. Christians and Muslims are all part of the same family. Same God, same human race.

The importance of taking the time to know our neighbors, to engage in true dialogue with one another, to teach and learn from each other, is often lost in our increasingly disconnected world. But when we highlight these connections, when we make the most of teachable moments to reach across divides, we dwell together as one and invite God's lavish blessings—life for evermore!

Michael Berino
Former High School English and French Teacher
English Teaching Assistant
The Fulbright Program
Dakar, Senegal

What We Cannot Earn

Psalm 136:2–3[11]

O give thanks to the God of gods,
*   for his steadfast love endures forever.*
O give thanks to the Lord of lords,
*   for his steadfast love endures forever.*

I have often thought that God made me a mother because that is the best context through which God can speak to me in ways I understand. One lesson I have heard loud and clear: you and I can no more earn God's love than any one of my children can earn mine. The love is already there. What's more, there is nothing you and I can do to lose God's love, just as there is nothing my children can do to lose mine. I find that amazing! Even so, I learned this the way I usually learn, and that is through pain.

I was home after attending yet another friend's baby shower, feeling both empty and guilty. Empty because after four years my husband and I still had no children. Guilty because I truly wanted to share in the joy of my friend's pregnancy, but I could not. I felt jealous and selfish and so mad at God. Surely God heard our plea, so obviously God did not care.

Feeling stuck and sad, my husband and I soon jumped at the chance to move abroad for his job and leave our infertility frustration behind. As we were packing to go, the phone rang. And before I knew it, I was holding a baby boy in my arms. A ridiculously absurd sequence of events—which I have since come to recognize as God's calling card—had literally placed this infant in my lap through a brave young girl's gift of adoption. We named him Michael. What joy!

Michael did not do anything to earn his way into our family. We were head over heels in love with him. We still are, just as we love the four additional children God has given us. Nothing any of them do will change that. Our love will endure forever.

In the same way, God loves each of us. Friends, there is no lesson plan or assessment or class taught so well that it can earn you God's love. Nor is there a lesson plan or assessment or class taught so poorly that it can lose God's love for you. God's love endures *forever*.

Judy Madden
Faculty
Alliance for Catholic Education
University of Notre Dame
Notre Dame, Indiana

WHEN WE BOW DOWN

PSALM 138:2

I will bow down toward your holy temple;
I praise your name for your mercy and
faithfulness.
For you have exalted over all
your name and your promise.

While staying with a friend recently, I went to say good night and found her kneeling next to her bed with arms outstretched across the duvet. I first thought this was a show of exhaustion (I've collapsed in a similar fashion after a long day of teaching), but as I got closer, I realized she was praying. My family kneeled at nightly prayer when I was a kid, and I still kneel at Mass, but somewhere along the way I lost the habit of that posture in personal prayer. In this small moment with my friend, I rediscovered the beauty of kneeling as a physical echo of the fervent praise we owe to God but can't always articulate.

In the tough moments of teaching and life, it is a valuable first step—and a sometimes-necessary last resort—to put our students and ourselves in a good posture, place, or point of view to show reverence and openness to God's plan for our lives, as this psalm implores us. And so . . .

- We circulate the room to better see what's going on in our classroom, knowing the high probability that the one moment our back is turned, an adept sophomore will manage to make the hole puncher explode.
- We ask our students to SLANT (Sit up, Listen, Ask relevant questions, Nod, and Track the speaker), believing that even if they don't attend to the material, attending to others is a good habit to learn.
- We frequent football games and school plays to show our care for pupils who will drive us crazy come Monday.
- We shift our mental perspective on a disagreement with a parent or coworker in the hope that we might have more compassion for that other person.
- We keep showing up to relationships with others and God, being present and prayerful in the midst of monotony.

Today, may the Spirit inspire us to physically and mentally bow down before God, orienting ourselves so we better see Christ in our days and in those with whom we live and work.

Maria Lynch
Spanish Teacher
Regis Jesuit High School
Denver, Colorado

STARS AND DOTS

PSALM 139:13–15

You formed my inmost being;
you knit me in my mother's womb.
I praise you, because I am wonderfully made;
wonderful are your works!
My very self you know.
My bones were not hidden from you
When I was being made in secret,
fashioned in the depths of the earth.

Because you're mine. That's why you matter to me." The wood-carver spoke with such tenderness to his beloved wooden puppet. "I made you. And I don't make mistakes." How the puppet needed to hear it![12]

Punchinello, the wooden protagonist in the story *You Are Special* by Max Lucado, routinely attempted to earn stars from his fellow puppets. Whenever he tried to jump high like his peers, he would fall. Whenever he spoke, he would say something senseless. Instead of stars, the puppets gave Punchinello dots to represent his failures and his inability to fit into the norm. Punchinello felt worthless and insignificant.

But in fact he was special, a creation of infinite worth. He just needed the wood-carver to reveal that to him.

For many of our students, school can be a terrible struggle—reading, a laborious task; math, a frustrating chore. Like Punchinello, these children do not receive the stars they so eagerly seek. They feel they have failed and are covered in dots. This is where we teachers need to ask ourselves whether we have become too consumed with student achievement, too encumbered by academic standards, and too focused on stars and dots. When and how do we reveal to our students their own true worth?

Each of our students is "wonderfully made . . . fashioned in the depths of the earth." God distinctly shaped them, beautifully. God sculpted their "inmost beings" and carved out their purposes. As teachers, our job is to discover our students' gifts and talents and to help them do the same. Our job is to point them affectionately past all stars and dots and, like the wood-carver, assure them that God has made them special and that God doesn't make mistakes.

Through this noble profession, God uses us to uncover each student's true ability and worth. Here we can foster the sort of learning environment that empowers each of our students to grow and flourish. We are carrying out the work of Christ the Teacher, helping to mold our pupils into the masterpieces God intended them to be. Like Punchinello, our students are all carved in the image and likeness of their Creator. Let's make it known!

Ian Corbett
Third Grade Teacher
St. Charles Borromeo Catholic School
Sacramento, California

The Folks Who Show Up

Psalm 146:5–6

Blessed [those] whose help is the God of Jacob,
whose hope is in the LORD, [their] God,
The maker of heaven and earth,
the seas and all that is in them,
Who keeps faith forever.

One autumn morning several years ago, my husband, Mark, suffered a neurological episode while walking outside to fetch the paper. He was thirty-seven. The episode looked and felt like a stroke, which landed him in the hospital for one week and befuddled doctors for several more. The problem was finally diagnosed as a rare, non-life-threatening infection, and Mark was back to his old self in a matter of months. But the experience was scary and threw our young family into a tailspin for a while. What got us through it were the helpers—the folks who just showed up.

They showed up at the hospital, on our doorstep, and in the hallways at school. Neighbors swung by the ER with hugs and dropped by the house with casseroles; the kids' principal welcomed my home-schooled fifth grader to school for a week; the art teacher organized a giant get-well card class project. Friends and family called and made calls, translated medical jargon, and in one case flew halfway across the country to lend a hand. They were purveyors of God's love, proof of God's presence with us.

I didn't see this at first, as can happen when hardship comes calling. Recognizing God requires an eyes-wide-open outlook that's difficult to adopt when we are winced in fear. And I was afraid. "Where are you, God?" I prayed. "My husband is suffering. My children are scared. Where are you, God?" Not until months later did it occur to me: *there* was God—in that art teacher, that principal, those neighbors and friends.

In times of crisis, advised Mister Rogers, "look for the helpers"—in our homes and in our classrooms, in our schoolyards and in our own backyards. Helpers show us, when pain and fear make it easy to miss, that God is near. My family learned that one autumn years ago. Look for the helpers. In them our faithful God comes, again and again and again.

Ann Primus Berends
Associate Director
Education, Schooling, and Society
Institute for Educational Initiatives
University of Notre Dame
Notre Dame, Indiana

Ms. Brown's Calculus Class

Proverbs 1:7a

Fear of the Lord is the beginning of knowledge.

When I think of fear of the Lord, I think of Ms. Brown's high school calculus class. Not because the class felt like divine punishment or because I was afraid of failing or because I dreaded the inevitable math puns—experiences we typically associate with the word *fear*. Rather, the class engendered in me a sense of wonder. As understood by Christianity, this is the meaning of fear of the Lord. It is a heartfelt recognition of the greatness of God, a recognition that leads us to realize our own inadequacies and unworthiness in comparison. The result of such fear is not despair but rather awe, reverence, obedience, and the beginning of true knowledge.

Reverence and wonder were concretely embodied in Ms. Brown's approach to calculus. For her, writing an elegant proof or solving a complex word problem was not an act of brute human achievement but a window into the awe-inspiring structure of mathematics. Doing calculus was not about conquering numbers;

it was about learning to understand the beauty and power inherent in numbers, a beauty and power that point to God's own.

Often we think that acquiring knowledge means forcing an object (a frog, a poem, a calculus problem) to reveal its secrets, thereby overcoming the obscure mystery it holds. We become masters and manipulators of the object. When fear of the Lord is the foundation, however, knowledge becomes something acquired through humble attentiveness. The awe and reverence we feel in the presence of God teaches us that we are not the center of the universe. The pieces of knowledge we acquire always point to a greater mystery. So it was in Ms. Brown's class. Her greatest joy seemed to come not when we mastered a concept but when we recognized for ourselves the divine greatness that she saw so clearly through calculus.

True knowledge consists in allowing an object of study to draw us out of ourselves and into an appreciation of something that transcends us. Fear of the Lord teaches us a responsible deference that makes us listening and receptive learners. May all of us strive to cultivate and communicate this disposition.

Steve Calme
Former High School English and Spanish Teacher
Doctoral Student
Department of Theology
Marquette University
Milwaukee, Wisconsin

ARE WE LISTENING?

PROVERBS 2:1–2, 5

My [child], if you receive my words
and treasure my commands,
Turning your ear to wisdom,
inclining your heart to understanding . . .
Then you will understand the fear of the LORD;
the knowledge of God you will find.

A great teacher I once observed used to show her
students very explicitly how she wanted them to
listen. "Don't just listen with your ears; listen with
your eyes!" she would say as she walked around the
room, teaching her students to follow her with their
gaze. "Listen with your body!" she would add, model-
ing for students how to sit up straight and put their
hands in their laps. When she asked her students to
listen, they knew exactly what was expected of them.
She taught them how important the skill was and why
it would propel their learning.

As teachers, we are used to helping our students
listen to us. We are wired to think about our own voices. We plan what we will say and how we will deliver it.
We practice techniques to ensure that we can be heard

and understood by all. We even use tricks and games to confirm that our students are listening. This is all good and important work indeed. Yet the writer of Proverbs gives all of us teachers a simple but sage reminder: we must listen in order to learn. *We* must listen!

Amid our goal-setting, lesson-delivery, and classroom-management strategies, when and how do we stop to listen to our students? When and how do we stop to listen to God? Do we listen with our ears? Our bodies? Our *hearts*? If we turn our ears to wisdom and incline our hearts to understanding, counsels the writer of Proverbs, we will find the knowledge of God. We can only know who our students are, what they value, and how they learn if we instructors stop to pay attention and listen. We can only know who we are in Christ, what he values, and how he would have us learn if we stop to pay attention and listen to him— through his Word, in prayer, and in the lives of those we are teaching.

Let's embrace Proverbs's simple wisdom today and consider how we might listen to our students and to God.

Clare Roach
Faculty
Alliance for Catholic Education
University of Notre Dame
Notre Dame, Indiana

Notes That Last Forever

Proverbs 3:3–4

Do not let love and fidelity forsake you;
bind them around your neck;
write them on the tablet of your heart.
Then you will win favor and esteem
before God and human beings.

As a math teacher, I strive to provide my students with good notes, including leading problems, guiding examples, and thorough definitions that will serve as valuable resources when they study for assessments. I insist that students take their notes carefully and legibly, using loose-leaf paper and a math binder to keep everything carefully and chronologically organized. While many will never look at these notes beyond the initial transcription, this exercise plays an important role in the classroom.

Over time, students will lose track of their math notes. Some sheets will tear from the binder and immediately disappear into the compost pile found on the bottoms of lockers and backpacks. The most diligent hoarders may tuck pages away in a plastic crate at the end of the semester, planning to pull them out at some future point for nostalgia or reference. Yet eventually even these carefully curated archives will find their way to the recycling bin.

Contrast the ephemeral nature of these notes with the suggested permanence of the lessons in this passage from Proverbs 3. More than proportional thinking and algebraic reasoning, my students need a loving teacher and a faith-filled classroom. These will be the lessons that will equip them not only for this passing world but for the everlasting one.

Each day, I don a tie as part of my teacher outfit, a small sign of my professional responsibility to my students. Proverbs 3 indicates that faith and love are even more essential components of my wardrobe and are also to be worn around my neck for students to see. Once the pencil markings of formulas and diagrams fade, faith and love will remain on the tablet of their hearts, a tablet not easily edited or erased.

Years down the road, I pray that the sound of the "note" that resonates in a student's heart when hearing my name will be a function of the love I shared and the faithfulness I showed. These are the notes that "win esteem before God and human beings." These are the notes that last forever.

Dennis Rankin
Fifth to Eighth Grade Math Teacher
St. Peter Catholic School
Saint Paul, Minnesota

In the Belly of the Whale

Proverbs 3:5–6

Trust in the Lord with all your heart,
on your own intelligence do not rely.
In all your ways be mindful of [the Lord,
who] will make straight your paths.

I tend to be a bit dramatic, so it's no surprise that I used to compare my first two years in the classroom to, respectively, Good Friday and Easter Sunday. The second year was really good, but it required a pretty rough first year to get there. Recently I've taken to using another, *slightly* less dramatic story to describe my life during and after those years: Jonah and the whale.

During my first year of teaching, I, like Jonah to Ninevah, was sent to a new city. If not quite as difficult as preaching repentance to the Ninevites, I was still asked to do a very difficult job. And I often got mired in doing it all on my own without asking for God's help. By not turning to God in those challenging moments, I felt as if I were in the belly of a whale—or even that the belly of a whale would have been an improvement!

81

It is still difficult for me to make prayer and a reliance on God my first response to a challenging situation; I tend to rely on myself and a long night of work. Yet through the countless travails of teaching, I have come to see that apart from prayer, I become a bit like Jonah—exhausted, overwhelmed, and definitely wanting to be someplace else!

The beautiful wisdom about this passage from Proverbs is that it doesn't say that our acknowledgement of God will *change* the path God calls us to walk. Rather, it promises us that when we turn to God with all our hearts, God will make straight our paths in ways that we are not, on our own, able to see.

When we begin to feel alone in the belly of our whale—whether at the beginning of a new school year, during a long stretch of weeks lacking in holidays, or maybe on any given Monday—let us pray for each other. Let's pray that we will remember to stop and ask for God's guiding wisdom—not to change our paths but to show us why we are here and where we need to go.

Drew Clary
Former Middle School Math, Religion, and Social Studies Teacher
Seminarian
Moreau Seminary
University of Notre Dame
Notre Dame, Indiana

GOD'S GOODS

PROVERBS 3:27–28

Do not withhold any goods from the owner
when it is in your power to act.
Say not to your neighbor, "Go, come back tomorrow,
and I will give it to you," when all the while
you have it.

It is easy, perhaps even instinctual, for us to help a
student who is bleeding from a bounce pass gone
awry or to cheer for a student who finally does that
long division problem correctly. It's not so easy to ex-
tend kindness to the boy cutting the eraser you gave
him into tiny pieces or to the pair tying their shoes
together during Mass. It's not easy to offer patience
when you've repeated the instructions five times and
underlined the important parts in different colors and
yet the student still doesn't have a clue about what
she's supposed to be doing.

Being generous with the goods to which God's children have a claim—as any teacher, parent, or caregiv-
er can attest—is not easy. There are days when all we
want to say is "Go, come again later; after I've graded
all your assignments and gotten a good night's sleep,

then I will give you what you need." But we are not the ones who get to decide when someone deserves our generosity. God decided that everyone deserves it at all times, regardless of their actions. Even the boy who just kicked the student across from him as hard as he could. Especially him.

My dad always says he wished he had become a teacher because he believes it is the best way to impact the next generation for good. As teachers, we have been charged with that duty—to impact and educate our future. We are entrusted, in part, with the care of our students' hearts and souls, which are watching us all day long. In our choices to give good now or to say, "Come back tomorrow," we are setting an example for the way we want them to give at home, on the playground, and in their futures.

Through Christ, it is always in our power to give more. We were made for love, out of love, and to love with the command to offer it now—even to the student who just knocked that desperately needed coffee off your desk.

Rose Oldenburg
Fourth Grade Teacher
Nativity Jesuit Academy
Milwaukee, Wisconsin

Failure's Gift

Proverbs 11:2

When pride comes, disgrace comes,
but with the humble is wisdom.

Humility: a gift that often comes after we fail. When I started teaching, I was twenty-two, fresh out of college, in a new city, and ready to be the difference in my students' lives. I was eager to be the great teacher I knew I could be, full of best practices and new ideas. But during those early years, I found myself failing much more than succeeding.

My second year of teaching will always hold a special place in my heart. I survived my first year (barely) and began my second year with a sense of relief, knowing more or less what to expect. However, nothing I had learned up to that point could have prepared me for what I learned that year from a sweet little girl named Lilly. With her as my guide, I came face-to-face with my pride.

Lilly suffered from severe epilepsy and had mini seizures throughout the day. With both physical and learning disabilities, she struggled as a student. The talk among the teachers was to instruct her as best we could, realizing that some concepts would simply go over her head. As months passed and Lilly's grades hovered only slightly above failing, I found myself burning out on my efforts with her and focusing more on students I believed could grasp the material. I'd check in with Lilly, but I spent less and less time trying to teach her how to multiply or read a passage fluently. "Just stop," I would say to myself when I worried about how to teach her. "She's not going to get it."

In the spring, Lilly's parents and I met for one of our regular appointments. While we chatted, I remember impatiently thinking, *I have so much to plan to reach my other students. The year is almost over; your daughter is getting through it. That's all we can expect!* Then her mom turned to me and said, "Lilly is really trying hard for you. She loves you! Last night she even had the idea to practice perimeter questions with markers in the bathtub. She drew all over the tub, just trying to understand it! Remember, it just takes her a little more time."

I was deeply humbled by her words. Lilly was giving me her all, and I needed to give her my all, too. She might not master every standard, but she was giving it her best, and she deserved mine. Pride had blinded me to the gift of this child in front of me. Humility opened my eyes. Wisdom is often described in our scriptures as hidden, revealed to and by the most unlikely: the humble. From precious Lilly, the hidden gift of the vocation to teach was revealed anew to me. What hidden treasures remain to be discovered in the unlikeliest of our students?

Megan Kirkland
Fourth Grade Teacher
St. Vincent de Paul Catholic School
Elkhart, Indiana

Bringing Joy to the Heart

Proverbs 15:29–30

The Lord is far from the wicked,
but hears the prayer of the just.
A cheerful glance brings joy to the heart;
good news invigorates the bones.

I walked to the corner of my tiny office and knelt on the carpet, joining a group of nine high school seniors to celebrate the last day of the semester. An ecstatic Juan was on one side of me, bursting with happiness after getting into his dream college; the endearing Paul was on the other side, an eighteen-year-old boy who later would try to give me extra money to make sure that the cost of the day's treats hadn't left me strapped for cash. A simple picnic meal sat in the middle of our circle. But before a single person dove in, one of them said quietly, "We should pray."

With that, we—three cheerleaders, two football players, the student body president, the soccer player, the math whiz, the saxophonist, and I—joined hands and prayed, and my heart melted even as it quietly rejoiced.

In a world that often tries to find the will to hold on to hope, I wish I could spread the idealism of these high school students. These are young people who genuinely want to "bring joy to the heart and . . . invigorate the bones." They want to do good, love well, and make a difference. They are hope-filled teenagers who list their American dream as being able to support a family. Who care about the well-being of those around them—teachers and peers alike. Who insist upon praying before a shared meal of Buffalo Wild Wings, taco dip, and brownies.

I may teach my students reading and writing, but ultimately I hope I'm teaching them to know God and, more importantly, to love God. I hope that Christ's light shining in my cheerful glance brings joy to their hearts. And I thank God for how the light in their own glances brings joy to mine.

Anne Brusky
English Teacher
Marist High School
Chicago, Illinois

In the Vineyard

PROVERBS 16:3

Entrust your works to the LORD,
and your plans will succeed.

As educators, the fact that the lives of children are entrusted to our care presents a real sense of urgency. For many of the students we serve, we see the need to do whatever it takes to give them an excellent Christian education, right now! Amid this urgency, we are reminded to entrust our works to the Lord, who will make our plans succeed.

I had a hard time connecting with one particular student at school. I struggled to find what motivated her and knew her life circumstances and personal challenges presented an occasion for urgency. Over two years we developed a stronger relationship, but as I didn't see a dramatic shift in her behavior and approach to learning, I wondered whether my efforts had made any sort of transformational impact.

The following year she was an eighth grader and at the top of many classes, and she often encouraged her classmates to work hard and take learning seriously. I discovered that she had gone to a camp that summer, put her faith in Jesus, and come back with a whole new approach to life.

Did I have anything to do with this transformation? Did my efforts perhaps plant a seed?

Regardless of the answer to these questions, as her teacher I had started with what I believed about her human dignity and capacity to thrive. Thankfully, I did not work alone but in a vineyard with many others who shared these beliefs about her and tirelessly strived to build the kingdom. Because of this, I could delight in and trust the ways that God's work began in her—work that will continue through the hands of others.

Urgency and trust that the Lord will provide must simultaneously guide our work. Together we are called to shower our students with goodness, high expectations, revolutionary love, and the constant communication that we believe each child is made in the image of God. And then, in the words of Proverbs, we must entrust our works to the Lord. Whether or not we have any impact as individuals, we know that our plans will succeed because God is bearing fruit through our sacred work together.

Erica Vesnaver
Former Middle School Science Teacher
Associate Program Director
Alliance for Catholic Education
University of Notre Dame
Notre Dame, Indiana

Our
Common Bond

PROVERBS 22:2–4

Rich and poor have a common bond:
the Lord is the maker of them all.
The astute see an evil and hide,
while the naive continue on and pay the
penalty.
The result of humility and fear of the Lord
is riches, honor, and life.

This passage begins by noting that "rich and poor have a common bond." Alternate versions say, "rich and poor rub shoulders" or "rich and poor meet together." Could our classrooms provide more evidence of this message, especially the visual of rubbing shoulders and standing side by side? In a culture focused on noting differences and weighing inequalities, how might we reshift our perceptions and focus on commonalities? How might students who are perceived as poor add a layer of richness to our classrooms?

We know as educators that our language matters because the lexicon carries with it connotations and perceptions. To what extent does my limited human language associate "rich"—good behavior, solid grades, and high parental involvement—with advantage? To what extent does it associate "poor"—language barriers, cultural differences, and incomplete homework—with deficiency and disadvantage? While we do not rely on the descriptors of rich and poor in reference to our students, how often do we use similar words—gifted, struggling, outgoing, shy—to describe our students and the differences that we perceive?

The writer of Proverbs reminds us that the Lord is the maker of them all. In God's eyes, all students are equally loved, equally called God's children, and equally made in God's image. The great news extends to teachers as well. We are equally loved, equally made in God's image, and equally called to empower our students—regardless of outward differences—to claim their deepest identities as God's own. Proverbs reminds us, too, to look past our human language and perceptions about what rich and poor look like. I think of the example of St. André Bessette. The world regarded him as a simple doorkeeper—poor, fragile, sickly, and small. But God regarded him as rich in faith, large-hearted, strong in his devotion to St. Joseph, and a great saint who extended God's healing love to all, rich and poor alike.

Today may God guide our vision, and so our words, about what is rich and what is poor and assist us in seeing equality as God sees it.

Katy Lichon
Faculty
Alliance for Catholic Education
University of Notre Dame
Notre Dame, Indiana

THE DANCING STUDENT

PROVERBS 22:6

Train the young in the way they should go;
even when old, they will not swerve from it.

Class starts with prayer. That has always been a nonnegotiable in my classroom, and it serves an important purpose: to refocus our efforts on the Lord for whom we live and to settle our middle school selves down so we can also focus on some math and science.

My students come from a handful of faith backgrounds, so our prayer takes on a variety of styles. For one of my former students, however, one feature never changed: every day he would "Dougie" as he rose from his chair to begin prayer and again as he returned to his seat. I often wondered if he saw this class-starter as anything more than a miniature flash mob or calisthenics. Still, there was never a doubt in my mind or his that we would start class with prayer. As we sometimes discussed as a class, our personal relationship with our Creator was worth two minutes to begin our lesson.

One day, my dancing student returned from some absences and needed to take an important exam he had missed. I handed him the test immediately and sent him to another room to get started. Just as the rest of us were about to begin prayer, the door flew back open. I was prepared for another dance performance. Instead, he simply looked at me and said, "Can I stay to pray with the class?"

Absolutely! What a beautiful reminder that, as Proverbs promises, the things to which we give pride of place as classroom leaders really do have staying power. For me, this interaction was a call to hope that he and his classmates will not turn from the ways they're being taught in our schools.

Of course, this student's family is his primary educator, and the values they instilled in him for years played a much larger role than my classroom routines. But all of us can be encouraged. The team effort of families and teachers to instill practices and values in young lives can have a lasting—indeed, everlasting—impact.

Alec Torigian
Middle School Math and Science Teacher
Academy of St. Benedict the African
Chicago, Illinois

A Glimpse into Heaven

PROVERBS 27:17

Iron is sharpened by iron;
one person sharpens another.

A ny questions?"
    After an anticipatory pause, a dozen hands shoot into the air, eager to start the conversation. Temporarily throwing time management to the wind, I start calling names, knowing that the class discussion will inevitably stray far from the path outlined in my lesson plan. This is, without question, the best part of the job. Though it sometimes feels like letting the animals run the zoo, opening up the floor to broad discussion generates some of the most stimulating moments in the classroom, for me as much as the students.

There is a part of me that wants to cut off the questions so we can proceed to the next subject, and often I do. On some days, however, I just have to allow the conversation to heat up and boil over before we move on to the next lesson. After a particularly lively theological debate or an eye-opening science lesson, my students and I often observe, "Isn't God's creation awesome?"

Teaching is more than an earthly profession. It is a glimpse into heaven as students and teacher work together to indulge their curiosities and uncover the truth, through which they can come to know God. As God grants the gift of wisdom to us, it is our joyous duty to share it with each other, to hone each other's mind and spirit.

Naturally, such joy often escapes us in the more mundane parts of the day. Nonetheless, when these occasions occur—when eyes that had glazed over shine with fresh understanding, when struggling minds grasp a concept that has evaded them for weeks, when some new knowledge of the world captivates a young heart and reinforces newfound curiosity—we remember our purpose. With the delight of these God-given encounters as our fuel, may we carry on our mission to sharpen young minds while maintaining an attitude of growth, love, and joy.

Melina Lopez
Second Grade Teacher
St. Paul Catholic School
San Antonio, Texas

CALLED TO ADVOCATE

Open your mouth in behalf of the mute,
and for the rights of the destitute;
Open your mouth, judge justly,
defend the needy and the poor!

We schoolteachers and leaders carry out some of life's most meaningful responsibilities. Among other things, we educate, facilitate growth, teach rules, guide discussions, encourage curiosity, pick up trash, tie shoes, clean up spilled milk, and wipe away tears. We are not obliged to do these things; instead, we are called to do them. This is our vocation, and the Holy Spirit enables us to fulfill it with compassion, love, and faith in the image of Christ our Teacher.

Not only are we called to teach, guide, and encourage our students, but as Proverbs urgently beckons and then as Christ models, we are impelled to advocate for each student every day, especially those who, in whatever way, cannot speak for themselves. This allows us to help develop school cultures in which each child—regardless of ability—is acknowledged as a gift from God.

We must help the student with low muscle tone hold a pencil confidently. We must create new versions of assessments for the students who are nonverbal. We must develop alternate assignments for the student who struggles with anxiety and depression. We must reallocate funds to make our playgrounds accessible for those children with physical limitations. We must coordinate with outside professionals to install the hearing-assistive devices for the student who is hard of hearing, and we must differentiate instruction for each child on the autism spectrum.

We do this not because we have to but because we are called by our own Teacher to take advantage of every opportunity to make academic, spiritual, and social success a reality for all children. In the spirit of Proverbs and in the spirit of Christ our Teacher, we acknowledge each student's abilities, speaking out, judging justly, and defending the rights of the poor and needy—showing each how to succeed using respect, empathy, and love.

Martine Romero
Vice Principal
St. Madeleine Sophie Catholic School
Bellevue, Washington

All That Has Gone Before

ECCLESIASTES 1:9–10

What has been, that will be; what has been done, that will be done. Nothing is new under the sun! Even the thing of which we say, "See, this is new!" has already existed in the ages that preceded us.

As educators, we often believe that we've seen it all. But once we think that we have, something invariably happens in our classrooms to teach us that we have not.

I thought I'd seen it all when I heard boisterous cries from another teacher's classroom. The raucous shouting and laughter were enough to garner my attention and prompt me to find out what in the world was going on in there. Upon my arrival I was surprised to see the teacher chasing a student around and around the room, the other students egging them on. Before I could say anything, *splat*, both the student and the teacher went down, one right after the other.

I thought for certain the teacher was going to really let the student have it; the rest of the class must have thought so, too, because a hush fell over the room.

101

Then a miraculous thing happened: the teacher and the student both erupted in joyous laughter. Indeed, on that day I saw something I'd never seen before.

What was it about that teacher and student that allowed them to find the humor in what could have been a decidedly humorless event? I think Ecclesiastes, with its perplexing insight that ultimately there is really nothing ever new under the sun, hints at an answer.

As teachers we must always be conscious that we have a great history. So much has existed before us that affects what we teach, the way we teach, and how we relate to our students. We must also be fully aware that each of our students has a great history; their experiences, home lives, and social situations affect so much of what goes on in our classrooms. They, like us, are God's children whose lives are woven into the fabric of all that has existed before us.

When we remember our shared heritage and the unique history we bring to each new day, we might even find the ability to laugh with our students and ourselves in otherwise difficult situations. This laughter—which at its heart is compassion—is what will be passed down through the generations to come.

Brian S. Collier
Faculty
Alliance for Catholic Education
University of Notre Dame
Notre Dame, Indiana

WHEN KNOWLEDGE
INCREASES GRIEF

ECCLESIASTES 1:18

In much wisdom there is much sorrow;
whoever increases knowledge increases grief.

I have always found it interesting that the tree of which Adam and Eve were forbidden to eat was "the tree of the *knowledge* of good and evil" (Gn 2:17, emphasis added). In education, don't we consider knowledge to be a good thing? If we are Christian schoolteachers, aren't we committed to helping our students grow in knowledge of God, of themselves, and of the world?

If so, why does the book of Ecclesiastes warn us that "whoever increases knowledge increases grief"?

As I walked into class one early fall morning to talk to a student about her summer reading essay, I could see that she was close to tears. "I thought I had done so well, Ms. Shea!" she said. "I worked so hard on this!" I sat down with her and listened for a while before gently walking her through some of my comments on her paper. I encouraged her to fix her mistakes and resubmit the essay. Her eyes widened.

103

"But Ms. Shea, there is so much I have to do to make it better. I see my mistakes now, but I don't know how to make them right."

How many times have I felt that way in my own teaching? The more reflective you become as a teacher, the more you recognize the huge gap between what you are doing and what you *should* be doing. Although I have improved a lot since my first year, I am more aware than ever of my weaknesses. Knowledge, indeed, increases grief.

But there is hope: the grief that comes from self-knowledge can remind us how little we are and how much we need God.

Refraining from eating from the original tree of knowledge was an opportunity for Adam and Eve to offer God loving obedience. In our fallen world, we who now know all too well about good and evil are called to this same obedience. But we walk in the confidence that, in Christ, God has responded completely to our need for him. May we and our students always offer our increasing knowledge, with its accompanying grief, to Christ our Teacher, who can show us how to use what we know to grow in him.

Maura Shea
English Teacher
Bishop Machebeuf High School
Denver, Colorado

FROM SEASON TO SEASON

ECCLESIASTES 3:1–4

There is an appointed time for everything,
and a time for every affair under the heavens.
A time to give birth, and a time to die;
a time to plant, and a time to uproot the plant.
A time to kill, and a time to heal;
a time to tear down, and a time to build.
A time to weep, and a time to laugh;
a time to mourn, and a time to dance.

The classroom is a sacred space, for it is where teachers enter into genuine relationships with their students. As a middle school teacher, I never knew what a given day would bring, but I was always certain that when my students walked through the door, they would bring a range of emotions—laughter, tears, anger, joy, pride. Together for that one school year, my students and I would watch the events of our world, our school, and our lives unfold—seasons of planting and uprooting, seasons of mourning and dancing.

Together in that sacred space we would process what we saw. As my students came to me day after day with their variety of experiences and emotions, I grew to realize that I was a constant presence in their lives. Regardless of the range of their emotions or the events unfolding around us, I was their trusted teacher for this gifted period of time.

When we walk a year's journey with our students, not only do we draw closer to them but ultimately we draw closer to Christ. The challenge for us becomes how we help our students draw closer to him. When they need to be heard, how do we listen? When their friendships break down, how do we help build them back up? When they are lost or confused, how do we help them find the answers they are searching for? When their hearts are joyful, how do we teach them to dance, embrace, and love one another?

There is a time for every event under heaven. As God's plan unfolds around us and our students, we can be confident that we were brought into this sacred space for a reason. We will most certainly experience mountain highs and valley lows together. The beautiful thing is that we have each other on the journey. We can laugh together, cry together, and be there for one another as God is there for us.

Today, may we and our students draw closer to Christ through each circumstance, seeing his presence in every moment and trusting his plan for all our lives.

Melodie Wyttenbach
Faculty
Alliance for Catholic Education
University of Notre Dame
Notre Dame, Indiana

KAIROS

ECCLESIASTES 3:11–13

God has made everything appropriate to its time, but has put the timeless into their hearts so they cannot find out, from beginning to end, the work which God has done. I recognized that there is nothing better than to rejoice and to do well during life. Moreover, that all can eat and drink and enjoy the good of all their toil—this is a gift of God.

I visited a colleague's classroom not too long ago. Checking the time, I glanced up at the clock to see a sign that read, "The clock is working. Are YOU?" Even as a passive observer, I felt a slight panic. Was I working, really? Was I producing something to show for it?

Educators are well aware of the value of maximizing instructional time. Making procedures more efficient can save hours of class time over the course of a year, and we rightly say that every minute counts. There is so much with which we want to leave our students—so much material to cover, so many books to read, so many equations to solve.

107

Yet in our desire to offer our students everything we can, there's a tendency to get caught up in our teacher sense of time: the deadlines and the due dates. "There will be a quiz Monday." "Report cards come out Friday." "You'll want to make sure you know this before eighth grade!" The bell rings, the term ends, and we briskly move on to the next unit. And especially when the semester becomes frantic, we get frustrated when we feel that we or our students are wasting time.

Yes, our time is precious, but it's God's time that matters in the end. God has set eternity in our hearts and in the hearts of our students. In some cases, we can see the fruits of our labor in this life—the students who ace the tests, who go off to college, who come back years later and thank us. But more often, we cannot fathom the extent of the work God has done "from beginning to end." We think in terms of *chronos* ("The clock's working"), while God is more concerned with *kairos* ("God's time"). We're not saved by the bell; we're saved by God's Son. Education, then, is not a process only of edification but of sanctification —a process that recognizes our children are made for greatness—and we don't get to set the deadline for that.

The clock is working. And so should we. But let's not forget that in the midst of it all, God is working, too.

Dan Faas
Former English, Literature, and Religion Teacher
Curriculum and Staff Development Associate
Office of the Superintendent of Schools
The Archdiocese of New York
New York, New York

LOCKED DOORS

ECCLESIASTES 4:9–10, 12

*Two are better than one: they get a good wage
for their toil. If the one falls, the other will help
the fallen one. But woe to the solitary person! If
that one should fall, there is no other to help. . . .
Where one alone may be overcome, two together
can resist. A three-ply cord is not easily broken.*

Darkness surrounded me as I trudged across the
blacktop toward school, arms laden with bags
stuffed with papers waiting to be graded from the
week. A dim light from the front of the school lit my
path, and I felt the cool metal of my keys against my
hand. Stopping at least once on the short trek to re-
adjust my load, I opened the door to the school and
then the door to my classroom. Click. They both
locked behind me.

Locked doors found their way into my life during
my first year of teaching. And although locks are
meant to keep us safe, they can isolate us if we let
them. In those first few months, I often found that I
was so desperate to work on lesson plans and assignments—already stressing about the school day—that

I would leave my classroom door locked even when I was inside of it. I never thought to leave it open. It would take a teacher, student, or my principal knocking for me to open the door, and even then I let it swing shut behind me when our conversation was done. Click. Locked. I liked it that way.

Although I was stubborn about my door at first, the students, families, faculty, and staff of my school beautifully persisted in drawing me into community with them. I don't know if they had read Ecclesiastes, but they certainly knew its powerful insight. In through my door came Maria, Julian, and Roberto, middle schoolers ready to try the math problems again. In came little Lydia, a pre-K student helping her mom clean the facilities after school. In came my colleagues, my principal, and my mentors, offering guidance and insight, a pick-me-up drink from Sonic, or copies from my mailbox. I began to realize how much I not only delighted in these people but how much stronger I was when I let them support me. My door was unlocked and open more and more often.

We are called amid our busyness and stress to be in companionship where one lifts up another, to open the doors in our lives and engage with each other. It is there that we see Christ in one another, and it is there—as Ecclesiastes promises—that we flourish.

Erin Rosario
Former Middle School Math and Science Teacher
Associate Program Director
Alliance for Catholic Education
University of Notre Dame
Notre Dame, Indiana

REJECT SELF-REPORT

ECCLESIASTES 5:1

Be not hasty in your utterance and let not your heart be quick to make a promise in God's presence. God is in heaven and you are on earth; therefore let your words be few.

Students tell us many things: "Mr. McEvoy, that homework was impossible!" "Mr. McEvoy, I really get this!" "Mr. McEvoy, that concept makes no sense!" However, the first technique any master teacher develops is to reject self-report. Students are often bad at assessing their own abilities. Therefore, in my classroom students complete an "exit ticket," some problem or task that assesses their mastery of the day's objective.

While they do, it is crucial for me to stay quiet and observe. If I swoop in to help, I have distorted the accuracy of the assessment. It takes time to develop the ability to hold back—to take Ecclesiastes' wise advice to let my words be few—and allow the students to work. Eventually, I hope they gain confidence to attempt each task independently and honestly, knowing that I will guide them through any mistakes they make.

I think it is the same with God and each of us. We are notoriously bad at assessing our own status as God's holy people. We may be overly confident in our relationship with God and fail to see our need for guidance and mercy. We may be overly scrupulous or discouraged and despairing, thinking that God's guidance and mercy are never meant for us. Or we may be in-between, requiring some help beyond ourselves to see more accurately where we stand and how to navigate our mistakes.

Occasionally when my class is completing an exit ticket, I pause to observe one student help another with the problem. While I know that the student's work is no longer independent, I allow it because I want the students to know that they can look to each other for help. In fact, I designed the seating chart to foster these discussions.

Ecclesiastes' wisdom reminds me that sometimes God may pause to lovingly observe us seeking answers. No matter what the task, when troubles arise we can be confident God will guide us. In fact, God may have seated us right next to the person who is best equipped to help us along the way.

Tim McEvoy
Math Teacher
Bishop Kenny High School
Jacksonville, Florida

GOD OUR POWER

ECCLESIASTES 9:10A

Anything you can turn your hand to, do with what power you have.

God calls us to work. In a classroom, we are never without work; there is an endless supply of tasks for us to do and, in the spirit of Ecclesiastes, we endeavor to do them with the power we have. However, there is a risk at stake that teaching will transition from vocation to grind, from heartfelt commitment to dreaded obligation. To guard against this risk, we must remember that God does not expect perfection but effort. And we must dedicate everything we do to God, who is the source of our strength.

When I started teaching, I felt the constant need to work harder and devote more time to schoolwork, which meant I had less time to devote to prayer. My goal was to be the perfect teacher. And because my mind-set was that my work was my prayer, I spent more hours lost in the world of my laptop and lesson planning than lost in intentional time with God. As my prayer life suffered, so did my interest in my work, and my perspective on my vocation began to change from lofty endeavor to drudgery.

Over time, I realized that God was not calling me to be a perfect teacher. God was calling me to be myself and to teach with all the power I have, to go all in, and to leave nothing on the court or, in my case, in the classroom. I began to see that my work is not my prayer and made my relationship with God a priority again. I fought the temptation to give up when a teaching strategy or a part of my prayer life fell flat. I took hope in the fact that, in both cases, marginal gains aggregate over time. And every day I practiced returning it all—my effort, my struggles, my work—to God.

God calls us to work with all the power we have, power that alone will never be enough for the job. We must constantly, prayerfully rely on God, remembering "that the one who began a good work in [us] will continue to complete it until the day of Christ Jesus" (Phil 1:6).

Mike Murphy
Fifth Grade Teacher
Nativity Preparatory School
Boston, Massachusetts

In the Café-Gym-Otorium

Ecclesiastes 9:17

*The quiet words of the wise are more to be heeded
than the shouting of a ruler among fools.*

Tulsa, Oklahoma, where I began my teaching career, has a vibrant food scene. From down-home barbecue joints to hip food trucks serving *banh mi*, the culinary options are diverse and, almost without exception, delicious! However, even the most elegant steakhouse in all of Oklahoma pales in comparison to a humble kitchen on the city's west side. There—nestled in the corner of a ramshackle building nicknamed the "Café-Gym-Otorium"—is where the legendary Mr. Bailly lives.

Both Franciscan sisters and students at Saint Catherine School marvel at Mr. Bailly's chicken-fried steak fingers, and parish volunteers will regale you with stories of his quick wit. He calls himself the Ragin' Cajun in honor of his roots, and his wide smile and deep belly laugh are prodigious. As you can guess, the man leaves an impression! But it is *how* he leaves an impression that has most affected me.

Whether cooking lunch for students or preparing a free community meal for the surrounding neighborhood, Mr. Bailly puts his heart and soul into his craft. He always explains that his objective is to provide the best dining experience possible no matter the audience, and he never loses sight of that. The setting is simple and the menus far from gourmet, but he treats the task with radical reverence. The generosity of spirit filling this humble cafeteria speaks much louder than any five-star review ever could.

Jesus delivered his prophetic words and works similarly. Christ did not produce esoteric encyclicals with arcane ideas accessible only to a select few; he taught in simple parables. Nor did he spend his time in the grandest temples or palaces but in the streets and synagogues. Jesus knew that the most authentic and grace-filled experiences are with people. Jesus lived with the radical intention that we experience God's love most vibrantly in the gritty work of everyday life.

Indeed, as the author of Ecclesiastes instructs, true wisdom is found not in the loudest voice or in the most sophisticated person or in the most exotic locale. Rather, true wisdom is discovered each day through women and men who are quietly bringing about the reign of God in authentic and ordinary ways. It is John the Baptist in the desert. It is Dorothy Day in the slums of New York. It is Mr. Bailly in the Café-Gym-Otorium.

Will Newkirk
Former Third Grade Teacher
Special Projects Coordinator
Institute for Educational Initiatives
University of Notre Dame
Notre Dame, Indiana

A Self-Fulfilling Prophecy

Ecclesiastes 10:10

If the ax becomes dull, and the blade is not sharpened, then effort must be increased. But the advantage of wisdom is success.

As teachers, we can become swallowed up in exhaustion and find ourselves frantically trying to get through each day. We fail to sharpen our blades and thus undermine our efficacy as teachers. We become overwhelmed and stressed by competing responsibilities, stacks of grading, lesson planning, and student misbehavior.

This was exactly my experience during a particularly challenging week when, as a new teacher, I had my first truly embarrassing moment. A colleague, looking concerned, asked me if I was okay. I quickly responded that I was fine and followed up with a defensive "Why do you ask?" He told me he had heard me yelling at my second graders on the schoolyard during dismissal.

I was embarrassed. Raising my voice at seven-year-olds was not part of my philosophy of teaching, and it wasn't who I wanted to be as a teacher.

However, I was later grateful for this uncomfortable moment because it prompted me to reflect deeply on how and why I had failed as a teacher that day.

Teachers wield incredible influence over the students in their care. In my harried attempts to get everything done, I lost sight of this truth. I allowed exhaustion to drive my actions, and in doing so, I became an instrument of fear and humiliation in my classroom. My reaction to student misbehavior relied on brute strength, and it compromised my students' trust in me.

Ecclesiastes reminds us that the cycle of stress and exhaustion is part of a self-fulfilling prophecy. I wasn't prepared, which led to a stressful day, which made me exhausted, which jeopardized my planning. I wasn't the victim of these circumstances but a partial creator of them. Because I did not proactively prepare my classroom for learning, I resorted to sheer effort alone at the expense of compassion and effective pedagogy.

As teachers we are called to be disciples of hope to our students. That hope begins with our preparation for each day. Sharpening our blades frees us to meet the needs of our students not with force but with care.

Frankie (Mary Frances) Jones
Faculty
Alliance for Catholic Education
University of Notre Dame
Notre Dame, Indiana

THE GREAT SAGUARO CACTUS

ECCLESIASTES 11:5

Just as you do not know how the life breath
enters the human frame in the mother's
womb,
So you do not know the work of God,
who is working in everything.

Some varieties of bamboo grow at the astonishing rate of thirty-six inches per day—an inch-and-a-half per hour. As the sun rises in the sky each morning, the bamboo's green shoots race heavenward. For most other plants, however, growth is slow and imperceptible to the human eye. What the bamboo shoot can accomplish in an hour takes the great saguaro cactus nearly two years to match. Growth, change, and progress begin internally, proceed slowly, and remain hidden from notice. By the time we can observe the growth, we have long missed the stages of development deep within and the inner blossoming that precede change.

Teachers face the reality of hidden growth every day. The seeds planted in the classroom germinate in the human heart with little regard for our well-laid schedules, instead preferring to operate in God's time and according to God's mysterious ways. For this reason—as teachers and as Christians—we are first and foremost a people of hope. We not only seek the lost sheep; we nurture them, too, trusting that our efforts on behalf of the knowledge and love within our students will bring to fruition the good work God has already begun. God plants, teachers nourish, and with time and grace lives are transformed.

Teaching requires that we remember that God is at work both inside and outside of time. Out of nothing God created the day and the night, the stars, the sun, and the moon. So, too, God creates us and our students. The joy of teaching lies not in our approaching each day with the certainty that we will witness all that God has in store for our students' growth but rather in surrendering all that we have and are to the great mystery of God's creative work. Teaching, in the end, is an act of faith in which one nourishes the seeds God has planted in the human heart and, with hope-filled patience, waits for them to blossom in the warmth of the Son's light and love.

Fr. Andrew Nelson, S.T.L.
Former History, Reading, and Theology Teacher
Parochial Vicar
Good Shepherd and Holy Family Parishes
Berlin-Gorham, New Hampshire

ROOTED IN LOVE

SONG OF SONGS 8:6A, 7A

Set me as a seal upon your heart,
as a seal upon your arm;
For Love is as strong as Death. . . .
Deep waters cannot quench love,
nor rivers sweep it away.

What does it mean to love our students? Last year, I returned to teaching after taking a six-year break to enter religious life. Being new to my school and a bit rusty on the job, I vowed this simple goal: to love my students though everything else might go wrong.

During the year, I often asked for God's help in achieving this goal. I began to see that, as I bumbled my way through new material, I was loving my students. As I helped the struggling ones with homework after school, I was loving them. As I encouraged them to reflect on their behavior or academic progress so as to mature and grow, I was loving my students.

Then something unexpected happened. When summer came and I prayed through my experiences that year, I realized that I had spent most of the

124

time focused on love as *doing* for my students. What this scripture passage helps me remember is that I am made for more than *doing* love. Rather, I am also made to *be* love—to be compassionate toward others, to be grateful for their presence in my life, to be committed to my relationships with them.

What does it mean to love our students? In addition to all that I do for them, I have found that loving my students includes heartfelt concern for their well-being. It includes gratitude for our daily interactions in the classroom. It includes prayers of thanks for their successes and prayers of supplication for their various needs.

Teaching is hard, but I believe that being rooted in love in this way helps me to face each day's challenges with joy. "Deep waters cannot quench love, nor rivers sweep it away."

Gregory Celio, S.J.
High School Social Studies Teacher
Bellarmine Preparatory School
Tacoma, Washington

Fifteen Hundred Decisions

Wisdom 7:7

Therefore I prayed, and prudence was given me;
I pleaded and the spirit of Wisdom came
to me.

A teacher recently approached me declaring, "Did you know the average teacher makes fifteen hundred educational decisions in *one* school day?" With that many decisions to make in a workday, it is a wonder we accomplish anything well and no surprise that we find ourselves exhausted by the day's end!

This is why any time we do God's work—whether in our homes or schools—we must remind ourselves to follow the author of Wisdom's advice and pray, and then pray some more! Whether making fifteen hundred decisions is fact or fiction, surely we can agree that we need prudence and wisdom to guide the countless choices we make on behalf of our students, our families, and ourselves as Christians called to serve.

A few verses later in Wisdom, the writer asks for the "unfailing treasure" of wisdom, acknowledging that "those who gain [her] win the friendship of God" and that gifts "come from her discipline" (7:14). As a pilgrim people following God's lead, we must strive to grow in such discipline, praying for wisdom as a habit and then an instinct that shapes every moment.

In our morning prayers, we ask for wisdom in all that awaits us. In conversation, we invite God's presence with a quick "Come Holy Spirit"—powerfully transforming difficult meetings, fostering breakthroughs with challenging student situations, mending disagreements among colleagues, or guiding our school community through trying times. At the end of the day, we ask the Lord for prudence in determining what to leave for tomorrow, enabling us to be truly present with loved ones waiting for us at home.

Continually praying for and discerning God's wisdom in all matters of life is a discipline that is both transformative and freeing. When we surrender our many decisions to Christ—who knows us best—we encounter the one who takes on our burdens, who never disappoints, and who is our truest friend in answering every prayer for our good in his time.

Heather Mehring Grams
Assistant Principal
Saint Vincent de Paul Catholic School
Denver, Colorado

WHAT WISDOM BRINGS

WISDOM 9:1–4

God of my ancestors, Lord of mercy,
*   you who have made all things by your word*
And in your wisdom have established
*   humankind*
*   to rule the creatures produced by you,*
And to govern the world in holiness and
*   righteousness,*
*   and to render judgment in integrity of heart:*
Give me Wisdom, the consort at your throne,
*   and do not reject me from among your*
*   children.*

The first time I observed a teacher in the class-room, the class was out of control. One student was especially disruptive and made me feel sorry for the teacher. Yet as wild as the situation was, I was impressed by the teacher's kindness and understanding toward his students. At the end of the day, I encouraged him, saying that I admired him for the patience and love he showed—especially to the students who challenged him. I promised my prayers for both him and his students.

A few months later, I went back for a visit and prepared myself for the madhouse. I was in for a surprise! When I walked through the door, the disruptive student politely greeted and welcomed me to the classroom. He was attentive, stayed seated, and even raised his hand to ask or answer questions. He was not perfect, but he had made so much progress. The atmosphere had become peaceful, and the students were learning.

What brought about the change in this class? It was the same teacher, the same group of students. I believe wisdom brought the change through the love of the teacher for his students. Wisdom, as this passage reveals, taught this teacher mercy and gave him the gift to govern "in holiness and righteousness, and to render judgment in integrity of heart."

Wisdom is a gift that God gives us when we quiet ourselves and open our hearts in prayer. We may not even know we are asking for it, but God knows our need for it. Through wisdom, God gives us a broad understanding that we are connected to everyone as brothers and sisters. This prayer in the book of Wisdom opens our ears to hear God's call to serve the world in holiness and justice. Wisdom helps us to look upon others with the love and compassion of

Jesus. Wisdom enables us to be God's unconditional love.

Pray for the gift of wisdom today, and discover how it will change you and open you to love God with your whole heart and soul and to love your students as yourself.

Fr. Joe Carey, C.S.C.
Chaplain
Alliance for Catholic Education
University of Notre Dame
Notre Dame, Indiana

A MYSTERIOUS
BALANCE

WISDOM 11:22–23

Indeed, before you the whole universe is as a
grain from a balance,
  or a drop of morning dew come down upon
  the earth.
But you have mercy on all, because you can do
all things;
  and you overlook sins for the sake of
  repentance.

All middle school teachers know that discipline can be tricky with adolescents. "Wait, why didn't he get detention?" "How come I got in trouble but she didn't?" "It's just not fair!" I am constantly considering the balance between justice and mercy. If I am merciful, am I seen as an inconsistent pushover? If I am just, am I seen as a loveless, inflexible dictator?

In contemplating these questions, my mind always wanders back to a college volunteer experience I had at a small, under-resourced Catholic school in Minneapolis, Minnesota. When I arrived in Ms. Cruz's room one day, I began working with David on his math homework. Unfortunately, David was having none of it. Defeated, I sat next to his blank math assignment as he wandered off to enact various shenanigans while "sharpening his pencil."

Noticing something was amiss, Ms. Cruz approached him and, given her Iron Lady reputation, I knew justice would be swift. I had seen her give David a detention before, so I was floored when instead of punishing him she crouched next to his desk, looked him in the eye, and said, "David, I've noticed you're having a rough day. Is everything alright?" Slowly, his tough façade melted under the patient gaze and empathy of his teacher.

Ms. Cruz truly understood the paradox of justice and mercy as balanced by love. She wasn't a pushover at all. Instead, she was merciful as the Lord is merciful. Even as she maintained the general order so necessary to effective education, she overlooked David's sins that he might repent and open his hurting heart to her.

God is not a pushover, nor is God an inflexible dictator. My own perception of justice and mercy as mutually exclusive must change because mercy may require the corrective discipline of detention some days and the disarming patience of listening other days. Mercy requires whatever will lead our students to repentance. May the Lord, who can do all things, give us the wisdom to discern this mysterious balance.

Ali Coffman
Middle School Language Arts Teacher
St. Hubert School
Chanhassen, Minnesota

Purified Gold

SIRACH 2:1, 4–6

My child, when you come to serve the Lord,
*   prepare yourself for trials. . . .*
Accept whatever happens to you;
*   in periods of humiliation be patient.*
For in fire gold is tested,
*   and the chosen, in the crucible of humiliation.*
Trust in God, and God will help you;
*   make your ways straight and hope in God.*

Whether you're a young teacher or a seasoned veteran, there is nothing that sends a jolt of adrenaline through your body faster than spotting your principal peeking in through your classroom window. Why is she here? Did I forget something? Are we doing anything engaging right now?

For my third-grade classroom, these visits always seemed to happen at the most inconvenient times. One day rings in my memory with particular clarity: just as a set of prospective parents peered in to see if our school might be the right fit for their child, a student angrily knocked over his chair in the back of the room, my well-intentioned lesson plan quickly fell apart, and I realized I had far too many ungraded papers strewn across my desk. Perhaps a day of your own comes to mind.

At such times, when feeling a deep sense of failure and humiliation, I am aware of the incredibly personal and vulnerable nature of teaching. While our students are at school, we are responsible for them. We put ourselves out there every day for their sakes, and our efforts can go terribly wrong. It is difficult to bounce back. It is exhausting to think about showing up for school the next day. It is hard to keep trying.

But we do. We do not stop teaching, and our response to moments of failure and humiliation shows our students what it is to trust in God's love and mercy. Jesus knew humiliation: his people turned against him, he was left alone to suffer in a garden, and he was placed on the Cross like a common criminal.

Through humiliation, Jesus speaks to us: "Stand up! You are loved. You are forgiven. I trust you. You will be even better through this." The powerful reality in the imagery of this passage from Sirach is that gold, when heated, first melts and only then is purified. In those inevitable moments of humiliation, we may lose our form, but we are purified and re-made by the master craftsman. Rejoice! God makes all things new.

Patrick Graff
Former Third Grade Teacher
Doctoral Student
Program for Interdisciplinary Educational Research
University of Notre Dame
Notre Dame, Indiana

The Problem with Planning

SIRACH 2:10

Consider the generations long past and see:
has anyone trusted in the Lord and been
disappointed?
Has anyone persevered in fear and been
forsaken?
Has anyone called upon the Lord and been
ignored?

Teachers love to plan. Each day is scheduled to the minute: 8:05–8:07, prayer; 8:07–8:10, bell ringer; 8:10–8:13, think, write, share. Even our bathroom breaks are planned: 10:15–10:18, speed walk to the bathroom, pray it's not occupied, and return before the next class arrives. The day goes on with each minute meticulously considered so that not a single one is wasted. We squeeze as much as we possibly can out of the day, recognizing that a great responsibility has been placed upon our shoulders—we are in charge of teaching the future!

But sometimes our day doesn't go as planned. Lessons flop. Students argue. Parents don't understand. Some evenings we leave our classrooms feeling as if our painstakingly organized day was a failure. At such times it is easy to feel lost and alone. We look around and wonder how God could have let our plans go awry. We forget that someone else is ultimately in control of our classroom. The Divine Teacher has the final say in what will happen each day.

The book of Sirach reminds us that since the beginning of time God has taken care of humankind. And so it calls us to trust even when our plans fall apart. When we look at the cross in each of our classrooms, we see the ultimate evidence of God's care, the ultimate reason to trust. From this we can gather strength and encouragement and the ability to live out our belief in Christ's resurrection. We can know that with him every failure may bring success; every defeat, victory. Consider the generations long past and see: the Divine Teacher will never forsake us.

Mary Forr
Middle School Latin, Religion, and Social Studies Teacher
St. Peter School
Washington, DC

Be Careful What You Pray For

Sirach 3:18–19

Humble yourself the more, the greater you are,
and you will find mercy in the sight of God.
For great is the power of the Lord;
by the humble [God] is glorified.

Be careful what you pray for," I am often warned. The moment I pray for humility, I nearly always find myself being humbled. This is when I am reminded of Jesus' quintessential prayer of humility: "Still not my will but yours be done" (Lk 22:42). Thankfully, as the author of Sirach writes, through my humility God is glorified.

How many times have I experienced humility while watching new teachers engage their classrooms with their talent and drive to be the very best for their students! Yet how many more times have I witnessed them suffering in that same humility, beginning with their first steps into the classroom. Prior to those first steps, they had rarely felt the sense of unknowing and inadequacy that comes while learning the intricacies of becoming a truly effective teacher. With Christ the

Teacher as their model, even the most talented and capable will be humbled.

Yes, the humbling begins as new teachers enter their first classrooms, but that is not where it ends. Even months later, they may feel ill-equipped and fearful despite all they have learned. This is the humbling that God wishes for these who are "the greater." Through their humility, Jesus takes the limelight off of their teaching and shines it most brightly on their Creator, Lord, and Friend. It is then that they begin to see that their work is not about them but about God and all that God can do through them. As they leave behind their focus on their own achievements and gradually realize the Master Teacher's focus on the students they are called to educate, they glorify God through their humility.

I have but a short time to assist these new teachers, to nurture them through their early days in the classroom. This in itself is a humbling charge. I turn for help to Christ the Teacher. To him alone be the glory.

Diane Maletta
Faculty
Alliance for Catholic Education
University of Notre Dame
Notre Dame, Indiana

An Anti-Gossip Classroom

SIRACH 4:29

Do not be haughty in your speech,
or lazy and slack in your deeds.

T his is an anti-gossip classroom!" I would exclaim
to the girls venturing into my room at lunch just
to talk badly about the other girls sitting outside. "It's
not gossip if it's true," they would argue. "Well," I
would retort, "if it doesn't need to be said, and it's not
anything nice, then I don't want it in my classroom!"

This battle went on for quite some time until one
day, as the whispers began yet again, one of the girls
stopped and firmly reminded the others, "Nope! Anti-gossip classroom!" I was overjoyed that the message, so wonderfully expressed in Sirach, had finally
been made clear: "Do not be haughty in your speech."

But Sirach's lesson was not over, for I noticed that
often I did not hold myself to the same standards I
held for my students. It was so easy to begin gossiping
about the apathy of what's-his-name, the annoying
behavior of so-and-so, or the ungratefulness of you-
know-who. This hypocrisy occurred even outside the
realm of speech and forced me to examine myself:

How often was I apathetic in my lesson planning? How often did I annoy those with whom I lived? How often did I fail to give thanks for all God had done for me?

"Do not be haughty in your speech, or lazy and slack in your deeds." Sirach challenges us as teachers to continually examine our own behavior. We want our students to grow up in a way that leads them to sainthood, so we set up boundaries, expectations, and guidelines to aid in their formation. If we, too, desire to be saints, we must construct our own parameters and let other teachers of wisdom remind us of them. Let us strive to lead an "anti-sin" life and strengthen our faith as we model Christ the Teacher in all we say and do.

Courtney Walker
High School Spanish Teacher
St. John Interparochial School
Plaquemine, Louisiana

The Risk of Silence

Sirach 5:10–12

Be steadfast regarding your knowledge,
and let your speech be consistent.
Be swift to hear,
but slow to answer.
If you can, answer your neighbor;
if not, place your hand over your mouth!

Silence does not come easily to me, especially in the classroom. I prefer to fill it with words—specifically, my own! When I am speaking, I am in control of what is being said. When I am silent, I am not.

To be silent in the classroom is to risk losing control to giggles and murmurs or, worse, to blank stares and crickets. All too often, to be silent in the classroom is to expose myself to the sinking sensation that I am trapped in the scene from the movie *Ferris Bueller's Day Off* when the teacher stands before his wordless students asking a series of questions, punctuated uncomfortably with "Anyone? Anyone?" At those moments, I am too quick to fill the painful void by answering my own questions. My students are off the hook, and so am I.

I may be off the hook, but I'm none the better for it because when I am speaking, I am not listening. And when I am not listening, I cannot hear. I cannot hear the questions that reveal what my students know and have yet to learn, and I cannot hear the insights that reveal what *I* know and have yet to learn. Teaching has shown me many things, including the truth that I do not have a monopoly on wisdom, knowledge, and understanding. These are gifts—gifts from God, my students and colleagues, my family and friends. And most often, silence provides the space in which they come to me.

These gifts come to me when I deliberate before answering questions and when I wait to hear what others have to say. They come to me when I put my hand over my mouth so that I can hear my students' questions, answers, and challenges or learn about my family's joys and sorrows at the end of a long day. And they come to me when I am quiet long enough to feel the tug of God's encouragement in my heart, calling me to listen more patiently, love more deeply, and teach as Christ taught.

Nicole Stelle Garnett
Faculty
Alliance for Catholic Education
University of Notre Dame
Notre Dame, Indiana

The "Eighth Sacrament"

Sirach 6:14–17

Faithful friends are a sturdy shelter,
whoever finds one finds a treasure.
Faithful friends are beyond price,
no amount can balance their worth.
Faithful friends are life-saving medicine;
those who fear God will find them.
Those who fear the Lord enjoy stable friendship,
for as they are, so will their neighbors be.

If there were an eighth sacrament, it would be friendship. For friendship so often makes the love of God palpably real to us—no small gift in the lives of teachers, who often spend hours a day with few peers in sight. Friends are the elixir of life. Friends make magic happen. I can only smile when I think of my life-giving friends, my soulmates. Like faith and family, how does anyone do it without friends? What a "sturdy shelter" my friends have been at points in my life when I have struggled physically, failed in the classroom, or experienced aloneness drifting into loneliness.

Many images of the centrality of friendship in scripture flood my mind: of Aaron and Hur holding up the arms of Moses, "the one on one side and one on the other," as he grew weary of extending them over the battlefield (Ex 17:12). Of Elisha asking for a "double portion" of his friend Elijah's spirit before he died (2 Kgs 2:9). And countless moments in the life and ministry of Jesus, including the gaggle of neighbors who brought their paralyzed friend to Jesus for help and, failing to gain entry because of the crowd, found their way to the roof, making their friend "tilt-able"[13] to lower him down in hope (Mk 2:2–4). What would it have been like for Jesus if every once in a while he hadn't been able to just relax mirthfully with his friend Lazarus as Mary quietly enjoyed the conversation and Martha bustled about the kitchen, grousing playfully, preparing Jesus' favorite meal and pouring him a cold one (see Lk 10:38–42)?

Perhaps on days when teaching seems only exhausting, friendship can be imagined as a deep well that offers support when we are weary, rest and celebration when we are joyous, an outstretched hand when we are stumbling—gifts of God to increase our delight. "Faithful friends are beyond price, no amount can balance their worth." Thanks be to God!

Fr. Tim Scully, C.S.C.
Faculty and Cofounder
Alliance for Catholic Education
University of Notre Dame
Notre Dame, Indiana

JUST BECAUSE

SIRACH 10:24, 28

The prince, the ruler, the judge are in honor;
    but none is greater than the one who fears
        God.
My [child], with humility have self-esteem;
    and give yourself the esteem you deserve.

In a teacher's day, there are a seemingly infinite number of opportunities to succeed or fail. Ask an insightful, thought-provoking question that engages your students? Success! Respond impatiently to a student who needs some extra guidance? Fail. We feel proud on our successful days, the days when we see our well-crafted plans facilitate great thinking and growth or when we compassionately respond to our students' needs. Other days feel like unending chains of humiliation. These are the days when our students' behavior seems out of our control, our lessons fail, and we wonder how we could have prevented all of these mistakes.

Such days can attack our self-esteem; they plant seeds of doubt about our gifts and our abilities. They make it easy to slide into the trap of connecting our sense of value with our professional successes and failures. Yet as Christians we believe that our value lies in our identity as children of God. God's unconditional love for us gives us our worth, and there is no success or failure in this world that can change it.

The children's book *Just Because You're Mine* by Sally Lloyd Jones captures the essence of this well. In the story, a little squirrel delights in showing his father everything he can do. When his dad tells him he loves him, the young squirrel assumes it is because of the skills and assets he's been showing off. "Do you love me because I'm fast? . . . Because I'm brave?" Of course the father's love isn't contingent upon any of these qualities. He tells his child, "I love you just because you're mine."[14]

We are worthy of God's love simply because we are God's creations. God instilled in us all of the gifts we need to bring compassion, grace, and mercy to the world. We honor our maker's wisdom when we remember that we are talented, capable, and infinitely valuable simply because we belong to God. Let us humbly receive our self-esteem from nothing less than God's unconditional love for us.

Michele Monk
Third Grade Teacher
St. Peter School
Washington, DC

THIN PLACES

Sirach 11:7

Before investigating, do not find fault;
examine first, then criticize.

In his first address to the faculty at my school, our
principal spoke of teaching as a ministry. As teachers, coaches, and counselors, he advised, we must
tread lightly and pray regularly. Why? He said, "In
this ministry we encounter many *thin places*—those
places or events in life where the dividing line be
tween the holy and the ordinary is very thin, to the
point that the ordinary becomes holy and the holy
becomes ordinary."

I still carry his words with me seven years later.
The notion of *thin places*—a beautiful ideal evoked
in Celtic spirituality—reminds me as a teacher and
coach that what I do is more than a job. It is a vocation, one that is led by the Spirit.

Ask me about "thin places" at certain times of the
year—early November or that week prior to Easter
break or after seniors receive their college accep-
tances—and I might describe them differently. Those
thin places are the days my patience has run thin. I

complain that student work is far from college prep and the battle with technology is no longer worth fighting. This kind of thin place doesn't offer me a healthy place to stand.

When I feel a bad spirit—one of cynicism, negativity, or disgust taking over in the classroom—I remember that I have traveled far from the thin places my principal spoke about. At such times, the book of Sirach offers welcome respite: "Before investigating, do not find fault; examine first, then criticize."

I believe if you look for something, you will find it. This simple passage reminds me what to look for, and my principal's advice reminds me how. Pray regularly. Seek the good. Review and examine with patience. Stand firm, but tread lightly. When we do, we will notice what we have encountered is more than ordinary. It is holy. Thin places abound.

Anne Stricherz
Theology Teacher
St. Ignatius College Preparatory
San Francisco, California

A STRATEGY UPENDED

SIRACH 13:22

When the rich speak they have many supporters;
though what they say is repugnant, it wins
approval.
When the poor speak people say, "Come, come,
speak up!"
though they are talking sense, they get no
hearing.

In the musical *Fiddler on the Roof*, Tevye sings, "It won't make one bit of difference if I answer right or wrong. When you're rich, they think you really know!"[15] While he envisions the respect granted by financial wealth, we see in the classroom wealth of other kinds—measured in popularity, class-accepted smarts, a new phone—determining whether people tune in. In any case, the wisdom of Sirach directs us away from this inclination to pay attention only to the well-off among us. Instead, it teaches us that one way we can preserve the dignity of those we tend to ignore—the poor, the outcasts—is simply by listening to them.

As a teacher who has always attempted to push middle school and now high school students to contribute to and collaborate in class discussions, I once felt it my duty to inspire the quiet students to speak up. Whoever they were, wherever they came from, I just wanted them to talk. Being able to speak to a crowd, especially a tough crowd, was life experience they needed, and my encouragement would help them know that I believed in them and they could believe in themselves.

I wasn't wrong, but like the second-best answer to a critical-reading passage, I also wasn't fully right. While each student does need to cultivate speaking skills, Sirach puts an equal spotlight here on the *audience*, and in so doing flips my strategy on its head. In other words, teach the audience how to listen first. If we focus primarily on how to speak, we are skipping a vital piece of the equation, which is how to be a member of the audience. In my classroom, I need to ensure not only that everyone speaks but also that everyone listens. The poor will speak if they know their voices will truly be heard.

David Bernica
English Teacher
Cristo Rey Boston High School
Boston, Massachusetts

LIKE SCOUTS

SIRACH 14:20–22

Happy those who meditate on Wisdom,
and fix their gaze on knowledge;
Who ponder her ways in their heart,
and understand her paths;
Who pursue her like a scout,
and watch at her entry way.

A drift as we are in a vast sea of activity and information, happy are those who meditate on wisdom. The modern condition would seem to be a paradox: while we move speedily, even incessantly, from home to classroom to practice to faculty meeting to late-night study session, we often end up going nowhere at all. We move without purpose, merely responding to the constant demands on our attention. But without purpose, our lives are only a shadow of what God intended for us. Happy are those who meditate on wisdom.

To meditate is not to be at a standstill. Just as paradoxically, the one who meditates on wisdom is on a proactive search, moving closer and closer to the truth. This search is everything. As Walker Percy writes, it is "what anyone would undertake if he were not sunk in the everydayness of his own life. To become aware of the possibility of the search is to be on to something. Not to be on to something is to be in despair."[16] Sirach tells us that we are meant to pursue wisdom "like a scout"—a zealous pilgrim on the road to a holy place.

Since the sixth century, pilgrims have both literally and figuratively pursued wisdom on the road to the Hagia Sophia—an Istanbul cathedral whose name means "Holy Wisdom." Emperor Justinian himself traveled there from Rome. It is said that, feeling ill, he leaned on one of the church's marble pillars and immediately felt better. Whether or not he was miraculously cured, echoes of Sirach shine through: happy the one who lies in wait at wisdom's entryway. In humble, faithful reverence we find respite, happiness, and eventually a deeper understanding of wisdom.

We are called to be active pilgrims in a world full of distractions, ardent scouts in a world full of paradox. On the journey, Sirach's message is clear: seek not to cover ground but to travel deep into your heart. Rest awhile there in reflection. Lie in wait at the entryway. Stop for a moment to notice the light as it shines in from above, illuminating a vast array of ancient marble columns of all colors. Happy are those who meditate on wisdom.

Iona Hughan
English Teacher
Tampa Catholic High School
Tampa, Florida

Every Kind of Student

Sirach 18:13[17]

*[The compassion of human beings] is for their
   neighbor,
   but the compassion of the Lord is for every
   living thing.
[The Lord] rebukes and trains and teaches them,
   and turns them back, as a shepherd his
   flock.*

Teachers are asked to meet the needs of every kind
of student, and there are many! It seems that the
gifts and needs and learning styles of our students become more diverse by the year. This passage from Sirach offers us a timely reminder about the compassion
of our Lord, which extends to "every living thing."

In our classrooms we are often drawn to the students who listen intently, follow directions the first
time they are given, and stay out of trouble. Like us,
they love learning. They make it effortless to plan
and easy to see the fruits of our labors. They are what
Sirach refers to as our neighbor.

Then there are the students who challenge us
and everything we know about teaching. They have

156

learned to hate learning, and they make it difficult for us to meet their demands in a large class filled with a variety of needs. There is no question that, despite our best efforts, every year we will find one or two—or more—lost sheep who have made their way to the margins of our classrooms.

Through those who test our tolerance and force us to question our practice, God constantly calls us to a broader compassion for every kind of student. Like shepherds to our flocks, we learn new ways to rebuke and train and teach. We show endless patience, devise creative plans and assessments, and understand that these students may not demonstrate immediate results—but they certainly will one day.

Catholic social teaching proclaims that we must put the needs of students who are at risk before all others: "The basic moral test of any environment is how our most vulnerable members are faring."[18] Sirach reminds us to love them well, too. The Lord asks us to care not only for our neighbors—our fellow scholarly students—but also for the ones who struggle. With the Good Shepherd as our guide, we are called to have compassion for every kind of student, for every living thing.

Lindsay Johns Will
Faculty
Alliance for Catholic Education
University of Notre Dame
Notre Dame, Indiana

THE BUSINESS OF FORMING SAINTS

SIRACH 21:19–21

To the senseless, education is fetters on the feet,
like manacles on the right hand.
Fools raise their voice in laughter,
but the prudent at most smile quietly.
Like a gold ornament is education to the wise,
like a bracelet on the right arm.

Is there any experience as uniquely inspiring—and fundamentally counter to the rhetoric on what is needed to resolve the challenges confronting K–12 education—as witnessing a high-performing Christian school in the midst of its work to put at-risk children on the path to college and heaven?

Several years ago, I had the opportunity to visit a Catholic school in the Rio Grande Valley. As my visit began, I spoke briefly with the school's principal, a spitfire of a woman who epitomized a sentiment that is often heard in some circles: her blood truly did seem to be in the school's bricks. At one point, she swept her arm across the panorama of the campus and commented, "All we're doing here is bringing these kids into deeper relationship with Jesus so that they can better recognize who they are and what they're called to be." For the remainder of my time there, I sat in awe of just how life-giving such work can be.

There's been an ocean of ink spilled on what's wrong with K–12 education, and much of it is written with tremendous hostility and pessimism. At times, the education reform movement has looked more like a battle over who is less wrong than a social enterprise to reimagine our greatest national treasure. It is easy to get lost in the miasma of competing theories of teacher accountability, cognitive outcomes, and fiscal effects and lose sight of what's at stake.

As teachers and leaders in Catholic or other Christian schools, we have the benefit of being granted a straightforward charge. We are in the business of forming saints. The only benchmark that really matters for our work is the sanctification of the children entrusted to our care. As I came to realize during that visit to the Rio Grande Valley, every day is another opportunity to help our students be who they are meant to be.

John Schoenig
Faculty
Alliance for Catholic Education
University of Notre Dame
Notre Dame, Indiana

Earthquake Insurance

Sirach 22:16

*A wooden beam firmly bonded into a building
is not loosened by an earthquake;
So the mind firmly resolved after careful
deliberation
will not be afraid at any time.*

It's strange to write, but the earthquake capital of the world is not in Japan, California, or some other place on the edge of a tectonic plate. It's Oklahoma. My beloved home has had more earthquakes in the past five years than any other location on Earth. It's a new phenomenon, so it has taken some getting used to. These earthquakes are front-page news, and they often headline the evening newscast. As a result, more people are buying earthquake insurance; schools are implementing earthquake drills; and more buildings are being fortified to withstand bigger tremors. Beams are being more firmly bonded to buildings so as not to be shaken loose.

Nothing shakes our lives quite like fear—fear of the unknown, health problems, failure, death. As teachers, we fear for our students and their well-being. We fear for their futures. Maybe we fear for our own futures. Maybe we look at our culture and fear where it is going. Make no mistake; there is much about which to be afraid.

Into that fear comes Jesus Christ who tells us over and over, "Do not be afraid." Do you believe him? If not, let us make the words our Lord gave to St. Faustina in 1931, "Jesus, I trust in you," a regular part of our prayer lives. Let us ask God for a deeper sense of trust. If we believe Jesus' words, we can be firmly resolved that he's in charge and that we have nothing to fear—not the ground shaking, not our futures, and not the futures of our students. Let us not be afraid! Jesus, we trust in you!

Rev. Brian O'Brien
President
Bishop Kelley High School
Tulsa, Oklahoma

WHERE WISDOM
MAKES HER HOME

SIRACH 24:8–9

Then the Creator of all gave [Wisdom a]
command,
and my Creator chose the spot for my tent.
[The Lord] said, "In Jacob make your dwelling,
in Israel your inheritance."
Before all ages, from the beginning, [the Lord]
created me,
and through all ages I shall not cease to be.

The Israelites were—like us and the children we teach—far from perfect. The Old Testament is filled with accounts of the Israelites doubting God, questioning God's love, even turning their backs on God. In the most difficult parts of the school year, I catch myself chronicling my (and my students') imperfections: I took too long to begin classes, structured my lessons poorly, and failed to make instructions clear to students, many of whom did not complete their homework, scored poorly on assessments . . . the list continues ad infinitum. No effort is ever enough, especially when after years of teaching I expect to have reached perfection as an educator. Still, like the Israelites, I am far from perfect. We are all far from perfect.

And yet, "the Creator of all . . . chose the spot for [Wisdom's] tent," saying, "In Jacob make your dwelling, in Israel your inheritance." God chose to house wisdom among the Israelites, who failed continuously, just as God later sent Jesus Christ to pitch his tent among us, fallen though we are. How easy it is to convince ourselves that we are not worthy of God's presence in our lives because of our imperfections. But Wisdom in Sirach, and later Christ in the gospels, knew that the humans they chose to live among would be hopelessly imperfect. And while that *does* frustrate God-among-us at times (a reminder that we still ought to strive for excellence), Wisdom finds her home with us because of our imperfections, not in spite of them. Wisdom is God's gift to us, not as an award for our successes but as a guide through our failures.

Therefore, we can view our imperfections and those of our students as vital reminders of our shared need for God's loving gift of wisdom. The imperfections in our lives need not lead to frustration—as they are often wont to do—but rather to love in action as we let wisdom build her inheritance among us.

Stephanie Mueth Pham
Twelfth Grade English Teacher
Cristo Rey New York High School
New York, New York

The Practice of Forgiveness

Sirach 28:2-4

Forgive your neighbor the wrong done to you;
then when you pray, your own sins will be
forgiven.
Does anyone nourish anger against another
and expect healing from the Lord?
Can one refuse mercy to a sinner like oneself,
yet seek pardon for one's own sins?

Showing mercy is the ultimate showing of love, and every day teachers are called to take up the challenge to bestow mercy on their students just as God bestows mercy on each of us. Merciful love is a transformative force that can become all-consuming. When we allow it to seep into our thoughts and actions, it can positively color the way we respond to difficult situations in our classrooms.

Loving our students well comes with many challenges. When they throw pencils at one another during the middle of a lesson, when they mockingly imitate us, or when the eyes of some roll so far back into their heads that we worry they will be permanently damaged, love and forgiveness may seem beyond our reach. We may be more prone to anger because, after all, we are human, and over time these transgressions can drive us to the breaking point. Upon closer examination, however, it helps to ask: Are we angry at the children for whom we care so much or at ourselves for our inability to love the way God mercifully loves us?

Healing, both for ourselves and for our students, begins to take place when we look past our frustrations and focus on forgiveness. When we consider how God has forgiven us, we can forgive ourselves for our shortcomings and forgive others for their transgressions. The practice of forgiveness transforms our own perspective from anger and negativity to mercy and love.

Oftentimes, the greatest teaching moments—for us and our students—arise when we need to respond and react in high-stress situations. When pencils are flying and eyes are rolling, we can model merciful love for our students. We can help them overcome frustration and move toward the healing act of forgiveness when we show them how.

Megan Otero
Middle School Science Teacher
Notre Dame School of Milwaukee
Milwaukee, Wisconsin

THE INFINITE IN THE FINITE

SIRACH 43:11–12

Behold the rainbow! Then bless its Maker,
  for majestic indeed is its splendor;
It spans the heavens with its glory,
    the hand of God has stretched it out in
      power.

In understanding science we understand just how magnificent God and his creations are, and we are able to create a better faith relationship when we acknowledge just how powerful God is. The more we are able to understand God's works, the more we are able to praise him. As a result of this knowledge and acknowledgment, we are able to teach others the glory of God based in science. This helps us to spread God's will of service and come closer to our Father as his children."

Amazingly, these words are from one of my eighth-grade students writing in response to the prompt "How do math and science lead us to God?" They point to what I have discovered is an indisputable truth in my time as a teacher: our God is one heck of a scientist and mathematician!

As a teacher, I am charged with the task of bringing my students to wonder at the sight of living, single-celled bacteria in what they thought was simply a drop of water; to awe at the understanding that the Earth—their whole world—is virtually insignificant in the scope of the entire universe; to marvel at the realization that the Fibonacci sequence occurs repeatedly throughout nature. I am called to lead my students to that moment of divine inspiration when they perceive the infinite in what they thought was finite, effectively changing their view of the world. It is my duty to lead my students to that precious instant where they can do nothing but exclaim with Sirach, "Behold the rainbow!"—not so much because they have advanced their own knowledge but because they appreciate the careful work of God all around them. Teaching, in this way, is nothing less than a collaboration with God, who constantly seeks to be revealed more fully in love.

May the Lord grant us this day the humility to work purposively toward God's end rather than our own. May our day's work be fruitful in drawing young souls toward the infinite in the finite, toward God's loving embrace!

Jessica Puricelli
Seventh and Eighth Grade Math and Science Teacher
St. Peter Claver Regional Catholic School
Atlanta, Georgia

To-Do Lists

Sirach 51:29–30

May your soul rejoice in God's mercy;
do not be ashamed to give [God] praise.
Work at your tasks in due season,
and in [God's] own time God will give you
your reward.

I don't know about you, but in my life of teaching, I have found it difficult to praise God for the mile-long inventory of strategies I want to learn about, lessons that I need to adapt, and topics I need to research. As with most teachers, this has led to a virtually bottomless to-do list. No sooner have I crossed out one item then another takes its place. I find it hard to rejoice in this season of life as an always-growing educator and hard to trust that in God's own time God will give me my reward.

As a college student, I had a different take on to-do lists. One year while studying abroad, I decided to make a list of one hundred things I wanted to do in my lifetime. I filled my One Hundred List quickly with items such as graduate from college, find my vocation, visit Rome, and write a book. As my life moved forward, I began to cross out items, each hatch-lined accomplishment signaling "success."

Somewhere along the way, however, my shrinking list began making me sad. I didn't feel nearly as complete as my nearly completed list suggested I should be. So I decided that each time I crossed one item off my list, I would add another. Among other things, the exercise became a revelation about my own evolution in the hands of God.

In these busy days, we must remember that, like my One Hundred List, we are incomplete and always growing toward fullness in Christ. Each event, experience, and relationship is transforming us into who God is calling us to be. Today, let us rejoice both in the items we cross off our lists and the items we add, each one representing something we can offer our students, our families, and our communities. Let us rejoice that, in God's hands, we are beautiful and holy works in progress.

Erin Wibbens
Faculty
Alliance for Catholic Education
University of Notre Dame
Notre Dame, Indiana

ABOUT THE ALLIANCE FOR CATHOLIC EDUCATION

The Alliance for Catholic Education (ACE), housed in the Institute for Educational Initiatives at the University of Notre Dame, exists for one purpose: to change the trajectory of children's lives and transform communities by strengthening, sustaining, and transforming Catholic schools. This closely knit, multigenerational program—honored by the White House, emulated by other universities, and growing in its impact and spectrum of services—engages people who are passionate about meeting the needs of faith-based, under-resourced elementary and secondary schools around the globe. Over the years, the program has become one of Notre Dame's marquee professional formation and outreach efforts. As of this printing, its participants and initiatives can be found in more than 1,600 Catholic schools in 116 dioceses across 44 states, serving more than 350,000 students.

ACE began in 1993 as a two-year service program (now called ACE Teaching Fellows), which offers committed college graduates the opportunity to serve as full-time teachers in under-resourced Catholic schools. ACE prepares its teachers in an innovative Master of Education program at Notre Dame that brings them to campus for two summers of intensive training and sends them out into classrooms during the school year. These teachers represent a diverse set of backgrounds and experiences from a broad variety of undergraduate disciplines. While teaching, they live together in small Christian communities and are supported throughout the year by both pastoral and academic staff at Notre Dame. Current ACE teachers, as well as graduates of the program and ACE faculty and pastoral team members, have written the majority of the reflections in this volume.

Since its inception, ACE has developed numerous kindred programs aimed at responding to several emerging needs within Catholic schools. As a result, ACE now offers a master's in educational leadership to provide Catholic schools with transformational leaders through the Mary Ann Remick Leadership Program. ACE also provides certification for teachers and school leaders striving to make their schools more inclusive of diverse learners through the Hernandez English as a New Language Program and the Program for Inclusive Education. Other initiatives, such as the Program for Educational Access and the

Catholic School Advantage Campaign, seek to help families, especially those from disadvantaged communities, access Catholic schools. And ACE offers several professional development opportunities, such as the Trustey Family STEM Initiative and the Center for Transformational Educational Leadership, which bolster the ever-increasing standard for academic excellence in Catholic schools while reinvigorating their Catholic culture and identity. Participants and faculty from all of these initiatives have also contributed reflections to this volume.

Notes

1. Dante Alighieri, *Divine Comedy*, translated by Henry F. Cary. vol. XX. The Harvard Classics (New York: P. F. Collier and Son).

2. Text from the leaflet Dag Hammarskjöld wrote for visitors to the United Nations' Meditation Room, which he designed.

3. *New Revised Standard Version.*

4. C. S. Lewis, *The Screwtape Letters* (New York: HarperCollins, 1942), 161.

5. John Paul II, *Salvifici Doloris*, sec. 19, accessed May 1, 2016, https://w2.vatican.va/content/john-paul-ii/en/apost_letters/1984/documents/hf_jp-ii_apl_11021984_salvifici-doloris.html.

6. Joseph Ratzinger, "Address to Catechists and Religion Teachers Jubilee of Catechists," in *New Evangelization: Building the Civilization of Love*, accessed May 1, 2016, http://www.ewtn.com/new_evangelization/Ratzinger.htm.

7. John Henry Newman and Frank Miller Turner, *The Idea of a University* (New Haven, CT: Yale University Press, 1996), 55.

8. Francis, as quoted by Gerard O'Connell, "Pope Francis Opens Holy Door Says: 'We Have to Put Mercy before Judgment,'" *America*, December 8, 2015, http://americamagazine.org/content/dispatches/

pope-francis-opens-holy-door-says-we-have-put-mercy-judgment.

9. Gerard Manley Hopkins, "Hurrahing in Harvest," Bartleby.com, accessed May 1, 2016, www.bartleby.com/122/14.html.

10. Peter, Paul and Mary, "Music Speaks Louder Than Words," by Harold Timothy Payne, Edgar B. Pease III, and Michael James Scarpiello, recorded February 16, 2010, on *Such Is Love*, Warner Brothers.

11. *New Revised Standard Version.*

12. Max Lucado, *You Are Special* (Wheaton, IL: Crossway Books, 1997).

13. Seamus Heaney, *Human Chain: Poems* (Great Britain: Faber and Faber, 2010), 16.

14. Sally Lloyd Jones, *Just Because You're Mine* (New York: Harper Collins, 2012).

15. Norman Jewison, Joseph Stein, Topol, Norma Crane, Leonard Frey, Molly Picon, Paul Mann, et al., *Fiddler on the Roof* (Beverly Hills, CA: Distributed by Twentieth Century Fox Home Entertainment, 2006).

16. Walker Percy, *The Moviegoer* (New York: Ivy Books, 1960), 10.

17. *New Revised Standard Version.*

18. USCCB.org, "Seven Themes of Catholic Social Teaching," accessed February 15, 2016, http://www.usccb.org/beliefs-and-teachings/what-we-believe/catholic-social-teaching/seven-themes-of-catholic-social-teaching.cfm.

Rev. Louis A. DelFra, C.S.C., is a priest in the Congregation of Holy Cross at the University of Notre Dame's Alliance for Catholic Education, where he serves as a faculty member and director of pastoral life. Fr. DelFra has also served as a middle school and high school teacher at Malvern Preparatory School in Philadelphia, and as an associate pastor and middle school religion teacher at Holy Redeemer Parish in Portland, Oregon. He received his undergraduate and master's degrees from the University of Notre Dame.

Ann Primus Berends is associate director of the Education, Schooling, and Society program at the University of Notre Dame and also works as its director of undergraduate studies. She has served as an associate director in the Alliance for Catholic Education; church director of in-house ministries in Nashville, Tennessee; project manager for education research at Vanderbilt University in Nashville; and coordinator of a literacy program at Highland View Elementary School in Silver Spring, Maryland. Additionally, she has worked for more than twenty-five years as a freelance writer and editor in both the public and private sectors.

AVE
Ave Maria Press

Founded in 1865, Ave Maria Press,
a ministry of the Congregation of
Holy Cross, is a Catholic publishing
company that serves the spiritual and
formative needs of the Church and its
schools, institutions, and ministers;
Christian individuals and families; and
others seeking spiritual nourishment.

For a complete listing of titles from

Ave Maria Press

Sorin Books

Forest of Peace

Christian Classics

visit www.avemariapress.com

AVE | Ave Maria Press
| Notre Dame, IN
A Ministry of the United States Province of Holy Cross